THE LANDLORD'S TROUBLESHOOTER

/

THE LANDLORD'S TROUBLESHOOTER

Second Edition

Robert Irwin

DEARBORN™
A **Kaplan Professional** Company

This publication is designed to provide accurate and authoritative information in regard to the subject matter covered. It is sold with the understanding that the publisher is not engaged in rendering legal, accounting, or other professional service. If legal advice or other expert assistance is required, the services of a competent professional should be sought.

Acquisitions Editor: Jean Iversen
Managing Editor: Jack Kiburz
Project Editor: Trey Thoelcke
Interior Design: Lucy Jenkins
Cover Design: Jody Billert, Billert Communications
Typesetting: the dotted i

Library of Congress Cataloging-in-Publication Data

Irwin, Robert, 1941–
    The landlord's troubleshooter / Robert Irwin. — 2nd ed.
        p.   cm.
    Includes index.
    ISBN 0-7931-3344-0 (pbk.)
    1. Real estate management. 2. Rental housing—Management.
    3. Landlord and tenant. I. Title.
    HD1394.I78   1999
    333.5′4—dc21   99-29568
                                                        CIP

Dearborn books are available at special quantity discounts to use as premiums and sales promotions, or for use in corporate training programs. For more information, please call the Special Sales Manager at 800-621-9621, ext. 4514, or write to Dearborn Financial Publishing, Inc., 155 N. Wacker Drive, Chicago, IL 60606-1719.

1. There are no acceptable excuses for late rent.

2. Always get cash (or cash equivalents).

3. Having no tenant is better than having a bad tenant.

4. Always be friendly with your tenants; never be their friend.

5. Don't insist that your tenants follow your lifestyle or family rules.

6. The only thing worse than a tenant who doesn't pay and moves is a tenant who doesn't pay and stays.

7. A clean rental helps attract a clean tenant.

8. The best way to avoid evicting a bad tenant is not to rent to that person in the first place.

9. Never buy rental property more than an hour away from your home or in an area where you would be afraid to go and collect rents.

10. Get everything in writing. Never trust your memory; no one else will.

C O N T E N T S

Preface **xi**

1. Advertising that Gets Results **1**
2. Finding a Tenant Who Will Pay On Time **13**
3. Avoiding Problems with Antidiscrimination Laws **23**
4. The Rental Application **29**
5. Leases and Losses—A Good Rental Agreement **39**
6. Dealing with Required Disclosures, Security, and Health and Safety **57**
7. Cleaning Up and Preparing to Rent **75**
8. Moving the New Tenant In **81**
9. The Walk-Through Inspection—Protecting the Deposit **89**
10. Keeping the Good Tenant Happy **97**
11. When the Tenant Damages or Doesn't Maintain Your Property **105**
12. Making Repairs **115**
13. When the Rent Is Late **121**
14. When the Tenant Won't Pay and Won't Move **129**
15. Eviction **137**
16. When the Tenant Abandons the Property **147**
17. Returning the Security Deposit **153**
18. The Friendly Move-Out **161**
19. Your Insurance Requirements **173**
20. Raising the Rent **181**
21. Should You Hire a Property Management Firm? **187**
22. Rentals and the IRS **191**
23. Converting Your Home into a Rental **199**
24. When You're the New Owner **203**
    Appendix: Landlord's Forms **209**
    Index **261**

PREFACE

The goal of the first edition of *The Landlord's Troubleshooter* was to quickly answer the most troublesome questions that landlords have. It was intended as a fast and easy reference—a problem solver.

That it succeeded is evidenced by the high praise it received from reviewers and the enthusiastic response of so many readers. However, times change and along with them the trade of being a landlord.

This completely revised second edition brings *The Landlord's Troubleshooter* up to date with the latest information that landlords need. In addition to keeping the solid advice of the first edition, it expands into areas such as new rules for disclosures and antidiscrimination. Further, this time I've put all the many forms at the back of the book (plus added many more) where they can be more conveniently located.

This book will tell you how to find the good tenants, how to collect late rent, what to do when a tenant damages your property, and what the alternatives are to eviction (as well as when and how to evict). It gets right to these and other issues that most concern landlords.

I've been a landlord most of my life and I know that when landlords have problems, they want solutions right now! This book will provide them whether you're a first-time landlord with a single unit to rent, or an old pro with an apartment building loaded with troublesome tenants.

This book is a troubleshooter. You don't have to read it from cover to cover to get benefits. If you want an ad that pulls, or need know-how to handle a security deposit, or even have a cranky tenant who calls you at odd hours, you'll find solid advice on how to handle it.

This troubleshooter has answers that worked for me and for many professional residential property managers as well. It's a book of landlord's answers to landlord's questions. If you're a landlord and are out there in the rental battlefields, it is your defense weapon. Use it to protect yourself and come out a winner.

Advertising that Gets Results

A—you've got a rental; B—you want a tenant. What could be clearer? But how do you get from A to B? How do you find just the right tenant? You *advertise.*

Most people think that advertising simply means placing an ad in the local newspaper. While that is a basic method of getting the word out about your rental, there may be other, less expensive, methods. In this chapter we'll look at all the possible avenues of locating the right tenant for your rental.

Hint: No tenant is better than a bad tenant.

THE SIGN

Don't overlook or downplay the importance of a sign on the property. Over the years, I've probably gotten a third of my tenants from a sign placed in front of the property (or in a window in the case of a condo).

A sign works well because prospective tenants who want to live in your area often are cruising it, looking for rentals. In many cases, the first day you put out a sign you'll get people stopping to ask about the property.

The sign doesn't have to be fancy: it just needs to get the message across. A typical rental sign may read:

```
FOR RENT
555-3465
```

You may, of course, add additional information such as the number of bedrooms and the price. I advise against advertising the price *on the sign.* The people who see the sign can see only the outside of the property (unless you're there to show it, it's locked up). You may eliminate potential tenants who think the rent is too high or too low based on the property's outside appearance. But, they can't know the real value until they see the inside.

Besides, I think putting the price on the sign cheapens the property. It's almost like saying that the price is the only reason to rent this property: not its design, size, cleanliness, or other outstanding features.

Caution: If you're in the process of painting or fixing up the property, you want to make it clear that its current appearance is not the way it will look when it's available to rent. Therefore, it's a good idea to put a date on the sign (for example: Available 6/30). This also alerts tenants who must move from their current home when they can move into your property. (See more on this below.)

THE NEIGHBORHOOD FLIER

The problem with just using a sign is that unless people happen to drive down your street, they won't see it. If your street isn't heavily trafficked, your sign alone won't do the job.

I create a very brief flier describing the property and make a hundred or so copies. Then I hire a neighborhood kid to leave one at the door of all the houses nearby, as well as post them in public places. (Be careful to instruct your delivery person to not put them in mailboxes—the Postal Service won't tolerate anything in a mailbox that isn't properly stamped.)

LANDLORD'S STORY

Several years ago I was trying to rent a house using a sign and a newspaper ad. After almost a month, I finally rented the property to a marginal tenant (by then I was desperate).

No sooner had the new tenant started moving in than a neighbor from the house behind mine (and on a different street) stopped by to say she saw the moving van and how sorry she was that she hadn't known my house was for rent. Her cousin and his wife were new to the area and looking for just the sort of house I had. He had a great job, they had great credit and—you get the picture.

Since then, I make sure that all the neighbors know when I have a property for rent.

Distributing and posting fliers assures that all the neighbors know the house is for rent and they can send any prospective tenants by. The flier can be handwritten or typed. Copying costs only about $5 for a hundred, and usually another $10 will get them distributed.

FOR RENT!

You can paste in a picture of the property
for greater impact

1234 Titus Street
3 Bedroom, 2 Bath
$750
Den, Fireplace, Repainted, New Carpets
Call 555-5465
Available 10/1

Putting the price on the flier is a good idea. While people can always call, letting them know the price up front helps them know if it's in their price range.

TOO SOON/TOO LATE

Timing is critical in finding tenants. Typically rents are due on the 1st or 15th of the month. Prospective renters shop for a new rental a few weeks before the rent is due. (Timing also is critical when placing your newspaper ad, as we'll see shortly.) So it's a good idea to get your fliers (and your sign) on display early.

BULLETIN BOARDS

You may want to tack up your fliers on bulletin boards at supermarkets, pharmacies, and other neighborhood centers. Some boards only allow 3 × 5 cards, so you may have to copy the information onto one of those.

Another, better, source can be company bulletin boards. Call and ask if you can hang your flyer on the board at the housing or personnel offices of local companies. Most will be happy to oblige. Sometimes it's a good idea to hang four or five fliers with a push pin. That way, someone interested can take one and leave the rest for other prospective tenants.

One problem with bulletin boards, particularly in public areas such as shopping malls, is that you're also announcing that your house is vacant to an element who may be interested in breaking in to have a party there, or to steal appliances, drapes, or whatever. Though probably a remote possibility in most areas, you may want to bypass bulletin boards for this reason.

ONLINE ADS

You may wish to use a service that offers online advertising for rentals. Sometimes these services not only refer prospects to you, but also screen them in advance.

Be wary of services that act as agents and want substantial fees for finding tenants. It's one thing to pay $20 to get your property advertised online, quite another to pay 5% of a year's rental to a service for finding a tenant.

In many areas there are also free online bulletin boards. You post a notice about your property and it remains there for a specified time.

Local real estate agents may be able to recommend these services. You may also use a search engine such as Yahoo! or Excite for rental housing. Be sure, however, to specify an area. You don't want to list your property in Boston on a St. Louis bulletin board.

To use such a service you will need a computer, a modem, and a service provider such as America Online or Microsoft Network—or someone who will post your notice and forward your "hits" (replies) to you. Your accountant might provide this service.

Another source for high tech bulletin boards may be found on local cable access channels. Sometimes as part of its public access service, a channel will allow a landlord to list a rental for a week or so. If your cable company provides this service, take advantage of it. It may give you just five seconds to flash a notice, but the novelty of seeing a rental advertised on a cable access channel could attract widespread attention, and find you a choice tenant.

LIST WITH AGENTS

Landlords sometimes forget that real estate agents not only sell properties, but also rent them. Real estate agents, particularly those in big offices, often have a steady stream of calls from tenants looking for rentals.

Agents like rentals because they sometimes can convert prospective tenants to buyers and landlords to sellers. Often an agent will take on your property and handle the rental for just the cost of advertising.

Some agents, however, will want to list your property on the Multiple Listing Service or some other cobroking exchange. This means that they will split a commission with another broker who may find a tenant.

Though this gives your property much more exposure, it is probably the most expensive method of getting a tenant. The typical fee is a full month's rent. That's right—you pay the agent (or agents) one month's rent to find you a tenant.

Of course, the agent may qualify the tenant and guarantee a tenant will stay for a specific period of time. If the tenant moves out early, for example, the agent may refund a part of the fee or may find a new tenant for free or at a reduced fee, depending on your contract.

In a tight market where there are few tenants and many rentals, you may want to consider this alternative. After all, you don't pay unless the agent finds you a qualified tenant.

FEE LISTS

Some real estate agents also put out a list of rentals, area by area. They charge prospective tenants a fee for this list, which usually is updated weekly. Because getting on the list is often free to landlords, there's no harm in having your property listed there.

NEWSPAPER ADVERTISEMENTS

By far the most widely used advertising medium for rental properties is newspaper classified ads. On some Sundays at the end of the month, the rental ads may cover many pages. That is a problem. Your ad is in direct competition with everyone else's in the newspaper. The other problem is the cost. Advertising your property in the newspaper can be very costly, perhaps the most expensive form of advertising you're likely to use.

Hint: Less is more when it comes to classified advertising.

Tenants, however, often look to the newspaper as their first source of information about rentals. Therefore, unless your signs or fliers worked very well for you in the past, you will be hard-pressed not to use classified ads. Your goal remains effectiveness and keeping the cost down.

EFFECTIVE NEWSPAPER ADS

To get the biggest bang for your buck, you must think like a tenant. What sort of advertising would a tenant read?

Which Paper?

Don't advertise in the big city paper. It costs too much and it covers too wide an area. Just like buyers looking to purchase a house, tenants look for location first. They often look specifically within a single residential development, even a much smaller area. Many big city papers cover downtown and all suburbs. If you pay for advertising that reaches people completely out of your area, you're wasting your money.

On the other hand, there are local papers, weeklies, journals, shoppers' guides (given away free), penny-savers, and so on. These are typically aimed at a very small area. If you were looking for a rental in a specific area, wouldn't you look in these first?

You can often find these papers at local grocery stores. Also ask the neighbors or the tenant who is moving out which are the more popular papers. Don't be afraid to advertise in a small paper or one that's filled with ads and not many articles. They are often the best sources of tenants for you.

How Big?

Don't believe the old maxim that bigger is better. When it comes to rental advertising, bigger just means costlier.

Think of it from the tenants' perspectives. They search for the best, least expensive rental they can find. Someone who takes out a display ad is saying, in effect, "I can afford to place big, costly ads, therefore, it stands to reason that I have to charge more for my rental!"

Prospective tenants tend to look for the smallest ads. So that's what you need to get. I rarely put an ad in a paper that has more than three or four lines. That's more than enough to get my message across.

How Often?

Run your ad as often as possible. However, pick and choose when to run it. And change it frequently. That's not as contradictory as it sounds. The idea is to run the ad when tenants are looking for space. As noted earlier, because most tenants move around the first of the month, they're not reading ads the first week or second week of the month. Conserve your money.

Either don't advertise early in the month or run a smaller ad. If you have your act together, you'll rent from the first to the first and advertise from the middle of the month *before* your property becomes vacant.

The best time to catch tenants looking at ads is the second half of the month. You can tell this is so because typically rental ads will be heavier then.

Don't run the same ad for more than a week. If you don't find a tenant by then, change the ad. Otherwise, those who are looking will remember your ad and say to themselves, "That place must be the pits—they can't get it rented!"

What do you do if you haven't found a tenant during the last two weeks of the month?

If you want to continue running newspaper ads, run the minimum ad—usually two lines. It's just enough to give you exposure. Then concentrate on the other methods I've detailed previously.

What to Say

The hardest part of placing a classified ad for most people is figuring out what to say. The problem is usually one of perspective—the landlord's versus the tenants'. Most landlords tend to write things they like about the rental instead of identifying what tenants will find attractive. For example, the landlord may like a small yard because of reduced maintenance problems, but tenants may look for a big one for their kids to play in. Or the landlord may be thinking of the new double-pane insulated glass windows he recently installed to save on heating/cooling costs while the tenant wants to know that there is clean carpeting and a laundry room. When you're working to put together the words for your ad, think only about what your rental offers a tenant.

What Tenants Want

What are tenant benefits? Here are some of the things tenants want to know:

- *Location.* Mention a desirable neighborhood or school. Is the rental close to shopping, buses, and/or highways?

- *Size.* List the number of bedrooms and bathrooms. Mention if the house or lot is oversized, or if there is extra space such as a family room or basement.
- *Amenities.* List the fireplace, spa, pool, appliances, or other desired items that go with the rental.
- *Cleanliness.* If the rental is newly painted, has new carpeting or drapes, or is especially clean, say so.

From the above list, one might think that an ad would have to be a dozen lines long to get all of the features in. That's not really the case, partly because just a mention will do and partly because there are commonly understood abbreviations. For example, here's an ad that has benefits from each category:

> Acacia Schools—3 bdrm. 2 bath,
> oversize fam. rm., spa, frplce.,
> just repainted. $975. 555-4321

Abbreviations

Here are some common abbreviations you can use to shorten (and thus reduce the cost of) your ad:

- bedroom: bdrm
- fireplace: frplc
- dishwasher: dshwshr
- townhouse: twnhs
- washer/dryer: w/d
- garage: gar
- large: lg
- small: sml

Don't be afraid to use abbreviations. Just be careful that the abbreviations you do use are understandable. For example, I was recently reading the rental ads in the local paper and came across this strange one:

Fr. Rt.—3b/2b, chc lct, $550. 555-8979

Does it mean "Free Rent" or "For Rent"? Is it three bedrooms or two? Does "chc lct" mean "chocolate"? (Actually, I think the ad meant to say, "For Rent—3 bedrooms, 2 baths, choice location.")

If an abbreviation will cause confusion, write out the word.

The Hook

Every ad needs a "hook." This is the word or words at the beginning that catch the readers' attention and lure them to read the rest of what you have to say.

Generally speaking, your hook should be the best benefit your rental offers. In the above ad, it was the location, but it could be almost anything. Here are some great words you can use to hook potential tenants who are reading ads:

- oversize house
- close to schools (or close in)
- 5 bedrooms (emphasizing size)
- room to roam (oversize lot)
- just remodeled
- freshly painted
- new carpets and drapes
- garden living
- quiet cul-de-sac

You get the idea. Pick out the biggest benefit to your reader and stress it.

Don't Be Afraid of the Short Ad

It is possible to get away with a single-line ad. Remember, the ad is already appearing in a rental section of the paper, often under a specific area and type of property (such as condo). For example,

---

New Paint—3bdrm/2bath, $875, 555-4993

If it's a competitive market, you likely won't draw many responses. Other landlords with bigger, more descriptive ads will command tenants' attention.

On the other hand, when the rental market is good for landlords, almost any ad will do—even one this tiny.

Don't Sell the Obvious

On the other hand, sometimes you have to go for the second-best benefit because the first is obvious. For example, your paper may list rentals by neighborhood or local area. Your biggest benefit may be that your property is in the choice Westwood area. Because you're already listed in Westwood, you don't need to say it again. List the next-best benefit. Maybe you have one of the biggest homes in the area, or it was just repainted. Go with that.

The Price

Always mention the price when you *don't* give the address. (Don't give the address in an ad, unless you or a manager are always there to receive lookers.) You not only want to get as many potentially acceptable tenants as possible to call, you also want to eliminate those who can't afford or won't want your property. Price is the great leveler.

Discounted Newspaper Ads

Consider the possibility of getting discounted advertising. The most expensive ad is the single day placement. Sometimes it only costs a few dollars more to run an ad for a week than for a day. Similarly, two weeks may be only a few dollars more than one. (I wouldn't run the same ad for more than two weeks as it will get stale and stop attracting callers.) Chances are you're going to have to run the ad for a week or two anyway, so why not sign up for it at the beginning and save money.

The same pricing holds true for lines. A single line is typically the most expensive ad. Often, three lines can be purchased for just a few dollars more than one.

Also, consider special sections. Sometimes papers will have deep classified advertising discounts for rentals that are below a certain price, for example, below $300 or below $500.

BEWARE OF OFFERING MOVE-IN DISCOUNTS

When the rental market is bad (there are more properties than tenants), landlords, particularly apartment building owners, will cut their prices and then offer move-in discounts. For example, ads may start appearing which say, "First Month's Rent Free!" or "Free TV To Move In!"

Some tenants may chase after these discounts. They stay a month or two—long enough to get the promotion—and then move on to the next desperate landlord. You don't want these tenants. You want a tenant who is willing to rent for a long period of time (at least a year). If you are in a really tight market, it's better to lower the rent and get a good solid tenant than try to "buy" a tenant with discounts.

In the final analysis, your advertising, whether it's a sign or a classified ad, is your entree to the world of tenants out there. It's your first step in getting just the right kind of tenant.

Finding a Tenant Who Will Pay On Time

Placing an effective ad is only the first step to finding the right tenant. If your advertising works, prospective tenants will call. The next step is hooking them on your property and qualifying them.

RESPONDING TO A PROSPECTIVE TENANT'S CALL

There's an art (if not science) involved with responding to prospective tenants over the phone. Master it and you'll have no trouble getting just the tenant you want. On the other hand, if you blow it here, you'll find yourself wasting time with unqualified prospects, and, worse, getting tenants who don't pay the rent. Get your phone response act together and you'll save all kinds of problems down the road.

There are three simple steps to handling the phones when prospective tenants call. (Note: It's important not to discriminate when talking with tenants. I'll discuss this more fully in the next chapter.)

1. ENCOURAGE THE HESITANT CALLER

Callers may be just a little bit nervous and/or guarded. Usually they want to find out as much information from you about your rental before giving you any information about themselves. They want to screen out rentals they aren't going to be interested in. They don't want to waste their time talking with a landlord with a dog of a rental who tries to talk them into renting something they don't want.

This hesitation does not mean you're talking to an undesirable tenant—quite the opposite. You're probably talking to someone who wants to find just the right property to rent. As with fishing, you're getting a nibble. Now, the art is to turn that nibble into a real bite.

Encourage hesitant callers. Be polite and answer their questions as fully and carefully as possible. Give the prospects enough information to get them hooked. Then reel them in with questions of your own.

2. SELL THE PROPERTY

Promote your property. *Sell* it to the tenant. After all, it's the only product you have. Prospective tenants will ask the following basic questions:

- How many bedrooms are there and how big are they?
- Does it have a large kitchen, family room, or yard?
- Is it clean?
- Does it have a big garage?
- Do you take pets?

They may, of course, also ask questions geared to their specific needs. If your property has a pool, they may ask if it has a separate fence and gate surrounding it—a real concern for tenants who have small children. They may ask if you have 220-volt electrical outlets in the laundry room because they have an electric dryer. They may ask if your house is near a particular bus route that they need to use.

The art here is to amplify your answers and then turn the conversation around into innocuous questions. After all, you're just as interested in qualifying the prospects as the prospects are in qualifying your property. For example, when telling about the number and size of the bedrooms in your property, you might say something such as, "It has three bedrooms, all good size. The master is 14 feet by 12 feet. Is that big enough for your needs? Do you have children who will need more room?"

Or you might respond, "The house is located near the L-123 bus line and there's also an I-405 freeway access nearby. Is that close enough to your work?"

Or you might say, "It has a large three-car garage, with three separate doors and openers. Were you planning to work on cars in the garage or do you have a lot of extra stuff to store?"

You get the idea. After you've established rapport by answering a few questions directly, you can begin to turn each answer into a question of your own. Soon enough you'll be learning as much about the tenant as he or she will be learning about your property.

Eventually, if the tenant seems happy with your description of the property and you seem happy with the would-be tenant's responses, work the conversation around to meeting the tenant at the premises. That way the tenant can see if he or she likes it and you can qualify the tenant further.

Hint: Remember, when a prospective tenant calls, the aim of your conversation should always be to get the tenant to the property. You can't sign a rental agreement over the phone.

Beware the "Professional Tenant"

Sometimes you'll get a call from someone who seems to know more about your property than you do. This tenant knows the area and the house, and insists that you are charging too much, but will consider renting from you for a lesser amount. In other words, the tenant wants a concession over the phone.

Beware of such tenants; they are nothing but trouble. You may indeed want to give rent or other concessions to get a particularly good tenant. But, you can't make that decision after one phone conversation or before qualifying the tenant in writing.

Tenants who want small concessions early on often want bigger ones later. They may be tenants who hop-scotch from landlord to landlord— just the sort you don't want.

3. QUALIFYING THE TENANT

Next, there's the matter of deciding whether you're even interested in showing the property to the tenant who calls about your ad. You need to have certain qualifying questions in mind ahead of time.

Hint: There are questions you must not ask because they fall under antidiscrimination laws. See Chapter 3.

First, how many people will be occupying the property? While you can usually determine the maximum occupancy of your property, you can't discriminate by refusing to rent to tenants just because they have children. On the other hand, you can refuse to rent to people who have pets or certain types of pets (but not seeing-eye dogs), and you can require tenants to have minimum cash and financial qualifications. You can get at least an idea of how your tenant fits into all of these categories over the phone.

If the caller doesn't have enough money to move in, doesn't want to move in when your unit is ready, has too many family members for the size of the unit, or otherwise is disqualified, you would be wasting your time to show them the property—you wouldn't want them as a tenant anyhow.

Minimum Tenant Qualifications

Here are some minimum qualifications that you may want to consider when a prospective tenant calls on your property:

- Willing to move in when your rental is ready
- Appropriate number of people in family
- Has the cash available to pay all rent and deposits
- Has no pets or only those pets you allow

LANDLORD'S DILEMMA

You need to know about the prospective tenants' financial condition, their ability to pay the rent, and if they have the cash to move in. On the other hand, you don't want to chase away somebody who's just calling over the phone by appearing to be too nosy in a delicate area. One solution is to state up front what's needed to move in. For example, after you've talked for awhile and otherwise prequalified the prospective tenant, you might say, "The total move-in is the first month's rent of $750 plus a $750 cleaning deposit, for a total of $1,500. Is that going to be okay for you?" If the would-be tenant says it's no problem, you can proceed to show the property. On the other hand, if there's hemming and hawing and asking if part can be paid now and the rest in three weeks, you should probably eliminate this tenant from consideration.

GET THEM TO THE PROPERTY NOW

As noted earlier, it's all for naught until the tenant actually sees the property and you see the rental application. So get the tenant to the property.

I may say, "You sound as though you'd like the property I have for rent. Why don't I meet you there in half an hour and show it to you? You can then look it over and see if it will meet your needs."

If They Hesitate

If tenants seem hesitant to see the property, particularly after you've chatted for awhile and they seem to like what you've said (and you like what they've said), ask if there's a problem.

At this point the prospective tenant might blurt out any number of amazing things such as, "Well, I didn't want to mention it, but I have a horse." Or, "You see, I'm having a fight with my present landlord about the three months I'm behind on my rent." Or, "I actually have seven kids, but I'm sure we'll all fit in your one-bedroom unit." Or, "I plan to run an auto body repair shop out of the garage; is that okay?"

If you don't ask, you won't know.

SEEING THE PROPERTY LATER: GET A NAME AND PHONE NUMBER

If you're going to show the property, particularly if you're not on-site, the least you want to know is that there's a reasonably good chance the prospective tenant will show up. If they're willing to give their name and number over the phone, it's a pretty good indication they'll meet you.

Besides, if they don't show, you want to be able to call and ask what happened. Or, you could be delayed and may need to call and arrange a different time. If they have a cell phone, as many people do these days, it makes things easier. (It's also a good reason why you should have one!)

Sometimes landlords are afraid to ask for a name and phone number from someone who just calls about an ad for fear of scaring them away. My feeling is that if a prospective tenant won't give you these basics, there's not really all that much chance they'll even show up to see the property.

GIVE OUT THE ADDRESS

Sometimes prospective tenants will say they are interested, but they want to drive by the property to see if they like the location and the neighborhood. Or you may have an interested prospect but you are not available to show it right then. They'll ask for the address.

I have no problem with this. In fact, I find it saves me a lot of time. If the would-be tenant has already driven by and seen where the rental is located, and finds it acceptable, I'm way ahead when they call back asking to see the property. I'm almost guaranteed they will show up.

Hint: The very best way to avoid tenants who pay late, who ruin your property, who need to be evicted, is to not rent to them in the first place. Rent to the right person and you shouldn't have any problems.

MEETING THE TENANT

First impressions are important, both on the tenants' part and on yours. Therefore, when you meet the tenants you should make an effort to look presentable and to be as personable as possible. After all, the tenants are judging whether or not they would want you as a landlord. If your appearance is poor, or if you don't treat the tenant respectfully, you'll do yourself great harm. Good tenants won't rent from you. And tenants who do rent from you will not be the type of tenants you want.

Here are two stories, both true, of two very different types of landlords:

LANDLORD'S STORIES

The Bad Landlord

Sarah met the prospective tenants dressed in her sweats. She had been on her way to the gym and their call interrupted her. She let them know she was inconvenienced.

She took them through the property and made sure they understood that she wouldn't tolerate any funny business. "I expect this place to be kept clean at all times. If you have a problem, I expect you to take care of it. It had better be a big emergency and you had better not have caused it before you call me. I don't want any parties and no more than one guest at a time. I live only three doors down, so I'll know.

"The rent is due on the first and you're outta here if it's not paid by the third. You pay for all the utilities including the water and garbage, and you take care of the garden in front. I've been taken by tenants before and I know all the tricks and I'm not about to be taken again, got it?"

Tenants got it very quickly. If they rented from Sarah, they'd be on their own if there were problems with the rental, but she'd be micromanaging and in their faces all the time. Sarah got a string of bad tenants who wouldn't pay and often messed up her property. She often swore that there just were no more good people in the world.

The Good Landlord

When Erma showed a property, she carefully explained that it had been cleaned, but anything not in proper condition would be taken care of before they moved in. Erma said she would take care of any repairs that were necessary, but it was their responsibility to call her promptly about them. If they damaged anything, of course, she would expect them to pay.

"I want you to consider this property as your home and treat it as if you owned it. I'll be available if problems arise, but I'm not going to be in your hair. I will come by occasionally to see if everything is okay, particularly in the first few months. After that, you just call me if there's a problem.

"The rent is due on the first and I have an automatic deposit service that I would like you to use. I'll pay for water and garbage service, and there's a gardener who will take care of the front yard. You'll be responsible for the other outside areas. I try to be extremely fair and I've always had good luck with tenants. If at any time there's a problem, come talk to me and we'll try to work it out."

Hint: It's better for the landlord to pay for water and a gardener to be sure that the yard is always in good shape. This makes it easier to rerent on a moment's notice. Paying for garbage ensures that there are no problems with the health department.

Erma wasn't lying when she said she had good luck with tenants. She always did. Tenants seemed to sense she was fair and reasonable and would not seek to abuse or take advantage of them. And Sarah got just the type of tenants she expected, too.

Avoiding Hubris

The moral to this story can be found in the ancient Greek word *hubris*, or false pride. The Greeks were very concerned about not showing hubris and if you're a wise landlord, you will be, too. Sarah's problem was that she believed that because she was a landlord, she was a class above the tenants. She showed this attitude; good tenants recognized it and stayed away.

Erma, on the other hand, saw being a landlord as simply business. She was not a class above the tenants. Rather, she was a businessperson offering a product. She needed a good tenant as much as the tenant needed a good landlord. Her fairness showed through, and good tenants recognized it and rented from her.

WHAT SHOULD YOU ACCOMPLISH WHEN YOU SHOW THE PROPERTY?

Be sure that prospects see all of the property, including the closets, the garage, basement (if any), and the yard. You want prospects to know what they are renting up front so later on, after you've invested a lot of time in them, they don't suddenly realize your place is not for them.

Hint: Don't try to oversell the rental.

Be sure to let the prospects know about things that might not be obvious such as schools, shopping, transportation, and the overall neighborhood. Tenants with children often want to know that other children are nearby. Tenants who don't have children may also be concerned about children nearby, but for different reasons.

Sometimes prospective tenants will want to rent after the first look. But not always. Many times prospects want to think about it, to check out other rentals, to talk amongst themselves. Allow them time to do this. Remember, you'll never be able to force someone to rent your property who doesn't want to, so don't try. Besides, being too eager makes some people suspicious that you're hiding something about the property and it scares them away.

On the other hand, you want to further qualify prospects. As the situation allows, question the prospective tenants about their ability to pay the rent, when they can move in, if the property is appropriate for them (too many for the unit?), what kind of pets they have, do they have a water bed, and so forth.

THE APPLICATION

Once you get a prospect who wants to rent, the next step is the rental application. I'll have more to say about that in Chapter 4.

CHAPTER 3

Avoiding Problems with Antidiscrimination Laws

A long time ago, landlords could rent or not rent to anyone for any reason at all. Today we have antidiscrimination laws in housing. These laws protect all of us.

For a landlord, however, the news is that you have to watch yourself carefully to be sure that you don't discriminate, even inadvertently. The penalties for discrimination can be severe.

According to the 1988 Fair Housing Act, you cannot refuse to rent to someone because of their:

- race.
- color.
- national origin or ancestry.
- religion.
- sex.
- familial status (including children under the age of 18 living with parents or legal custodians; pregnant women, and people securing custody of children under the age of 18).
- physical disability.

Discriminating on the basis of any of the above is illegal. This is federal law and applies everywhere in the country, including where you have your rental. It means you cannot use any of the above criteria to

- refuse to rent housing.
- refuse to negotiate for housing.
- make housing unavailable.
- deny a dwelling.
- set different terms, conditions, or privileges for rental of a dwelling.
- provide different housing services or facilities.
- falsely deny that housing is available for inspection or rental.
- for profit, persuade owners to rent or deny anyone access to or membership in a facility or service related to the rental of housing.

Additionally, if you have a "no pets" policy, you must allow a visually impaired tenant to keep a guide dog. If you offer ample, unassigned parking, you must honor a request from a mobility-impaired tenant for a reserved space near to the apartment, if necessary, to ensure easy access to the apartment.

And, if your tenant has a physical or mental disability (including hearing, mobility, and visual impairments; chronic alcoholism; chronic mental illness; AIDS or AIDS-Related Complex; or mental retardation) that substantially limits one or more major life activities, has a record of or is regarded as having such a disability, you may not refuse to let the tenant make reasonable modification to your dwelling or common use areas, at the tenant's expense, if necessary for the handicapped person to use the housing. You may not refuse to make reasonable accommodations in rules, policies, practices, or services if necessary for the handicapped person to use the housing.

If you do, the injured person can file a complaint with HUD (Department of Housing and Urban Development) and you could be subject to an investigation and severe fines.

HUD offers books and free brochures through their Fair Housing Information Clearinghouse that explain the law in detail. Its number is 800-343-3442. It also offers a free newsletter and has online help at www. hud.gov. Although designed primarily for tenant use, if you have questions on discrimination, you can call the HUD Housing Discrimination Hotline at 800-669-9777.

OTHER ANTIDISCRIMINATION ORDINANCES

Many cities, counties, and states have ordinances that add new classes to the list. You should check with your local housing authority or a knowledgeable real estate agent who specializes in rentals in your area to find out what these are. Some local ordinances include:

- *Educational status.* You can't discriminate because the applicant is a student.
- *Sexual preference.* You can't discriminate if the applicants are homosexual.
- *Occupation.* You can't discriminate regardless of what the applicant does for a living.
- *Medical status.* You can't discriminate regardless of an applicant's medical condition (for example, if one has AIDS).
- *Age.*

Finally, there are also ordinances that have been passed by some local governments that add special restrictions. Here are some examples:

- *Number of occupants per house.* You cannot rent to more than four adults (over 18 years of age) per single family unit.
- *Number of cars.* Tenants cannot have more than two cars per rental unit.

LANDLORD'S DILEMMA

With so many antidiscrimination laws on the books, how do you keep out the bad tenants (those who won't pay or might ruin your property) and get the good ones? The good news is that you are free to discriminate in those areas that are critical to getting a good tenant. Specifically, you can reject a tenant who has a bad tenancy record (been evicted, has a history of late payments, bad credit, etc.), who doesn't have enough income to make the payments, who doesn't have enough cash to move in, who has too many members in the family for the size of the property, who has a pet that would damage the property, and so on.

In other words, you can still go after the good tenants—those who make the rent payments on time and keep the place in good shape.

HOW MANY IS TOO MANY?

One area worth a special note has to do with the number of tenants you allow in your property. Federal law emphasizes that you can't discriminate by refusing to rent to families. On the other hand, local statutes and common sense might require that you limit the number of people you can have in your property. What are you to do?

The problem is that there are often no hard-and-fast rules. Building and safety codes usually only state the maximum number of occupants per room and frequently that's as many as a dozen! (Fire codes may be more stringent—check with them.)

HUD offers guidelines on occupancy and these usually translate to around three persons per bedroom (two per bedroom plus one).

Unless local codes specify the maximum and minimum of people you can have in your property, you have to come up with some reasonable rules of your own and apply them across the board. As long as you don't change them for each tenant applicant and they're reasonable, you should be okay.

RENTING TO FAMILIES WITH KIDS

An old landlord's maxim was, "Kids are great—in your place, not mine!" Kids may be hard on a rental. They tend to mark walls, stain carpets, scratch floors and doors, and so on. Many landlords would prefer to rent to couples without children.

While you can no longer discriminate against a family because it has children, you can limit the number of children you will allow based on the size of the rental. The fewer kids in the rental, of course, the less damage is likely to occur.

How many kids per rental? As noted earlier, this is a gray area. Some landlords arbitrarily use the guideline of a maximum of two children plus one adult per bedroom. On the other hand, if you have a four-bedroom house, would you want a family with four adults and eight kids living there? There are also considerations of how many bathrooms, the total living space, the size of the yard, and so on.

Note: There are certain "adults only" communities where, for example, any resident must be over 55 years of age. Generally speaking, these are allowed if all occupants (or in some cases at least 80 percent) meet this requirement.

CREATE A WRITTEN SET OF GUIDELINES

You may spend years renting properties and not experience any hassles. But rest assured, one day someone will challenge your rental policies and you will have to defend them. If you do, your best defense is a set of written guidelines, available to tenants who challenge you.

A good analogy here is the workplace. Lawsuits for discrimination, wrongful termination, and harassment (sexual and otherwise) are increasingly common. Yet one of the best protections a company has is a set of written guidelines or rules that it follows scrupulously. In your rentals, if you can demonstrate that you have a clear policy and that you adhere to it across the board, you are one step ahead in any discrimination case.

How do you write guidelines? It's simple. Write down exactly what qualifications you want for tenants of the property (without violating any of the antidiscrimination laws noted earlier) and follow them assiduously. If anyone challenges you, you can whip them out to show you weren't discriminating.

TYPICAL TENANT GUIDELINES

Your guidelines must be applied to all tenants. They may include:

- *Assets in bank* must be equivalent to two months' rent.
- *Checking account* must include at least one account established with a local bank.
- *Credit cards* must include at least two major cards.
- *Credit report* must show no more than two late payments in the past six months.

- *Income of applicants* must be $_____ (either a set amount or a multiple of the rent).
- *Loud noises* are unacceptable. Applicant must have no history of loud parties or noise after 10 PM or before 7 AM.
- *Maximum number of tenants* is four.
- *Personal recommendations* must be provided from at least two sources.
- *Pets,* except for one cat, are prohibited.
- *Previous history of rent payments* must show on-time payment.
- *Vehicles* allowed are a maximum of two cars per property.
- *Waterbeds* are not allowed.

GRAY AREAS

What should be apparent is that, with certain specific exceptions as noted above, there's a lot of gray area. For example, can you refuse to rent to a tenant who has a motorcycle instead of a car? The tenant may argue you can't, that you'd be discriminating on the basis of how a tenant chooses to get around. On the other hand, you might say that motorcycles are all right, as long as they are properly muffled and don't make more than a certain decibel level of noise (comparable to that of an automobile). Many modern motorcycles are elegant, quiet roadsters.

What you want to aim for is consistency and reasonableness. Follow those two guidelines and you shouldn't go wrong.

Hint: The guidelines are for you to follow. You don't need to post them for tenants. You should follow them without exception and be ready to produce them if need be.

The Rental Application

No one rental application is the best. And you don't necessarily need to pay a lawyer to create one for you. You can get a model form from a stationery store.

You want a form that asks the right questions. With the help of modern computers and a word processor, you can even create your own application in a short time. The application in the Appendix of this book covers the essential information you need.

Hint: Don't refuse a rental application to anyone who asks for one. You don't want to be accused of discrimination by refusing to give out an application. I offer everyone who comes to see the property a rental application, even if they don't seem interested.

Make the form succinct. You want it to include all the information you need, but not be so extensive that it takes hours to fill out. A good application should require no more than 10 to 15 minutes to be filled out. Be sure the prospective tenant fills it out *completely,* especially the section on previous landlords.

Hint: Be thorough when you check out the tenant. Never rent to people who don't fill out applications. Never rent before checking out the references and information.

MAKE NO PROMISES YOU CAN'T KEEP

The application is not just a formality. Never, ever rent to prospects without first verifying the information on the form, no matter how perfect they seem. Never tell prospects that the rental is theirs to have before you've finished checking them out. Later, if there's a problem and you don't want to rent to them, they can complain that you're discriminating because first you agreed to the rental and now you are refusing to honor it.

If there are two or more prospective tenants filling out applications at the rental property at the same time, don't imply that the first person who returns the application gets the prize. You want to rent to the most qualified tenant, not the fastest writer.

FIVE CRITICAL TENANT TESTS

Having prospective tenants fill out rental applications is only the first step. Now, you must check out the information. There are five critical tests that will determine if they are good prospects. If prospective tenants fail *any* of these five tests, I wouldn't rent to them:

Hint: Be certain that your application specifically allows you to check prospective tenants' backgrounds (by calling previous landlords), finances (by checking with their banks), and credit (by securing credit reports). If a prospect does not specifically give you the right to do this, you can't do it.

Test 1: Will the landlord before the current one provide a recommendation?

This is the most critical test of all. You're asking the person who is in the best position to know about this tenant. Note I recommend checking out the landlord *before* the current one. A current landlord will almost always give a favorable recommendation. If the prospective tenants are great, the last landlord will say so. However, if your prospective tenants are a problem, the current landlord is still going to tell you they are wonderful, just to get rid of them! Only the landlord before the present one is likely to give you a true picture. If the prospective tenants don't have more than one landlord in their history, pay special attention to tests four and five below. A savvy landlord will only say whether the person was a tenant and paid the rent promptly. You may, however, gather more info in an informal chat.

Test 2: Will they give up their pet?

As landlords know, pets can take a high toll on a rental. They can scratch, tear, urinate, and defecate on the property, all of which can cause thousands of dollars of damage. (One cat urinating on a carpet can destroy the carpet, the padding, and even the flooring underneath!)

Ideally, you would rent without pets. However, in the real world you must assume that most, if not all, tenants will have pets. Therefore, the only question is not will they have pets, but how many and what kind?

LANDLORD'S STORY

Hal refused to rent to anyone who had a pet. He figured it was the easiest way to go. Consequently, as soon as prospective tenants learned of this, they would tell him they didn't have any pets. However, almost invariably, a few weeks or a month after they moved in, a pet (or two) would appear.

As soon as Hal found out, he would go over, shout at the tenants and tell them to get rid of the pet or leave. Likely as not, the tenants would get angry and, after a few months, depart, often leaving the property a mess.

As a result, Hal lost a lot of rental time and spent a lot of money cleaning up his properties. He didn't have any pets—but he didn't have many tenants, either.

My suggestion is that you learn to live with the fact that tenants tend to have pets. Or be prepared to do a lot of shouting and evicting.

Once you come to accept pets, the real question is one of controlling the number, the kind, and their deportment. The first two are a function of the rental agreement, the last a function of the deposit. (A bigger deposit because of a pet often ensures that the owners take special care that the pet is properly behaved.)

After filling out the application area about pets, many prospective tenants will ask if you accept them. You can say something such as, "Yes, provided it's a small pet and only cats or goldfish (or whatever)." At this point the tenant may say something such as, "But I have three Dobermans. They are wonderful dogs, so well behaved, so clean."

They certainly may be. But it's doubtful they would have room in a studio apartment with no yard. In fact, it might even be cruel to keep them in such close quarters.

When you explain this to a tenant, he or she may say, "It's a shame. But I want this place. Okay, I'll get rid of them."

I have a good friend, a property manager for more than 25 years, who would say, "I'm sorry, but I would never rent to anyone who would get rid of a pet!"

The point, of course, is that pets are like members of the family. Almost no one will give them up. If they say they will, they are probably fabricating. Rent to this person and chances are within a few weeks or months those pets will be living there, too.

Test 3: Can they afford to move?

These days it can take a fair amount of cash to move into a rental. Let's say you are renting for $950 a month. Of course, you will want the first month's rent up front, plus a security/cleaning deposit. It wouldn't be unusual to ask for a deposit equal to a month's rent. Now the prospective tenant has to come up with $1,900. (If your lease requires first *and* last month's rent, that's another $950. The tenant now needs $2,850.) That's a fair bit of change for a tenant who is interested in renting a place for under $1,000 a month. If you charge an extra pet deposit, the amount due rises even further.

Nevertheless, I always insist that this money must be paid (in cash or equivalent) before a tenant can move in. Sometimes tenants will try to negotiate to pay the first month's rent right now and the security/cleaning deposit in two or three installments over the next few weeks. They just can't come up with all the necessary cash.

It's a believable explanation and in a tight market, you will be tempted to accept it. But just ask yourself, what good is a security/cleaning deposit that you haven't collected? Further, my experience is that a tenant who can't come up with the money now will have trouble coming up with it later on as well.

The tenant should pay the first month's rent plus security deposit (plus last month's rent, if applicable) in cash or with a cashier's check or money order. I will accept a personal check with the understanding that the tenant won't move in until it clears my bank, usually at least two or three days.

Test 4: Do they have sufficient income to make the payments?

This is like qualifying a person for a home mortgage. According to many property managers, you should be sure that the tenant's gross income is at least three to four times the monthly rent. That supposedly ensures they have enough money coming in to handle the rent. These managers even have formulas for income, expenses, bank savings, and so on that you can apply to a tenant to determine whether or not they will be able to make their monthly payments.

In my experience, however, these formulas don't always work. I've rented to tenants who had no apparent income, yet managed just fine with the rent. And I've rented to tenants who showed more than five times monthly rent in income, yet still couldn't make the rent payments.

Sticking to rent being not more than 25 or 33 percent of income remains a good approach. However, I also like to use a different option: intuition. Instead of using a sharp pencil and an arbitrary formula, I sit down

LANDLORD'S STORY

I once had a prospective tenant who said he was currently unemployed, in fact had been unemployed for the past 18 months. He had no regular income.

Naturally I was concerned and asked how he expected to make the rent payments. He proceeded to inform me that the reason he was unemployed was that he had been injured at work and had received a cash settlement of more than $200,000, which he had banked. He was happy to have me confirm this with his bank. He said he planned on living on the money for a year or two before getting a new job.

I rented to him and he stayed two years, paying right on the due date.

with the rental application form and a prospective tenant to whom I want to rent the property and ask something like, "Do you figure you'll be able to handle the monthly rent payments? Where will you get the money?"

Good tenants usually consider this a reasonable question from a prospective landlord and will often quickly outline their basic expenses including utilities, food and so on, their fixed expenses, and their income— "proving" to me that it will work. I really don't pay much attention to the "proof." The fact that they have a plan is usually enough. I just want to be sure they know where the rent money is coming from and they are confident they can find it. (I also check out their employer and bank account to be sure they aren't making money up out of thin air.)

Note: to be in compliance with antidiscrimination laws, you will need to be sure to ask the same questions and apply the same criteria to all tenants.

If tenants say they don't have much income, but do have a lot of cash in the bank, don't hesitate to confirm that with the bank. Have them sign a standard "verification of deposit" request and send it off to the bank (see the Appendix for a typical form).

If tenants say they are depending on income from their employment to make the rent payments, be sure the credit check you do (noted below) confirms their employment. If it doesn't, then use a "verification of employment" form yourself.

Hint: Be wary of tenants who don't have regular employment or a good explanation for their income, yet have plenty of cash with which to pay the rent and deposits. They may be selling drugs and may intend on using your property as a drug house. As a landlord, you can be held responsible for what goes on in your property. You may be forced to evict them. What's worse, under certain circumstances, you could lose your property by confiscation to the federal government without trial and with little recourse!

Test 5: Do they have a good credit and rental history?

You must have some idea of how prospects handle bills and about the only way you can find this out is through an independent credit and/or rental history check. (Your rental application must request that the tenant give you permission to make such a check.)

Many landlords feel that getting a credit report is a hassle and requires too much time. I don't. It may be confusing the first time, but after you've established a method for getting the report, it should be easy to do. Besides, the information it provides can be invaluable.

L A N D L O R D ' S   S T O R Y

Sally had never used a credit reporting agency for her tenants, yet had fairly good luck with her rental. She would call the previous and/or current landlords, check with the tenant's employer and bank, and let it go at that. But finally she decided to go with a credit report.

Imagine her surprise when the very first check she ran revealed that the prospective tenant had dozens of late payments and defaulted accounts. The prospective tenant's application looked perfect. Her employer verified her employment. The bank said she had enough money on deposit to move in. But, the credit report revealed she was a deadbeat. Needless to say, Sally now uses credit checks on all her prospective tenants.

The question is, how do you, as a single landlord, run a credit check and a rental history check?

How Do I Run a Credit Check?

There are numerous credit checking agencies in every metropolitan area (listed under "Credit Reporting Agencies" in the yellow pages), in addition to the three national credit agencies:

Equifax	800-685-1111	(www.equifax.com)
Experion	800-682-7654	(www.experion.com)
Trans Union	800-916-8800	(www.tuc.com)

A formal, written credit report from one of the major agencies usually costs anywhere from $35 to $50 and, thus, is usually prohibitively expensive for rental credit checks.

However, many local agencies have a special single service option designed just for landlords, where, for a much smaller fee (often only $10 or $20), they will do a minimal credit search. Sometimes they will only report back verbally.

Finally, many areas have rental or landlord associations (described below) that belong to a credit reporting agency and can run a check for you at a nominal cost.

Note: You can ask the prospective tenant to pay all or a portion of the cost of the credit report. Some prospective tenants will balk at this, while others will feel it's perfectly natural, particularly if the cost is only around $10 or $15. I never ask for the tenant to pay for the report. I'm only going to get a credit report on a tenant who I'm pretty sure I want and the report really benefits me.

Hint: If you turn down a prospective tenant and offer as a reason a bad credit report, you have to tell the tenant the name of the credit reporting agency, but not specifically what was bad about the report. The same may hold true for negative information from a former landlord or other third party.

Rental History Check

What can be even more revealing than a credit check is a rental history check. Today there are landlord associations in virtually all metropolitan areas. (Look under "Landlord Associations" or "Housing Associations" in the yellow pages.) Sometimes these associations are tied in to others within the state and even between states.

These associations receive reports of late payments and evictions from their members and then make this information available to their members. Sometimes you will have to join the organization to get a rental history check (which could be quite expensive with annual dues), but other times the association will make it available to you for a nominal one-time fee, provided you agree to provide information to them on your tenants.

If prospective tenants have a bad report on a rental history check, I would be very careful about renting to them. No matter what explanations are given, what tenants did to one landlord, they are likely to do to another.

LETTING THE TENANT KNOW

If the tenant passes the five tests, then you've got a winner and should rent to them. You need to call them back and tell them you're willing to rent to them, provided both of you can agree on a couple of areas. One of the most important is the move-in date.

Tenants will always want to move in at a time that's most convenient for them. And of course, they want the rent to start when they move in, not before. This, however, can cost you money.

For example, let's say that your property is available on the 1st of the month. However, you don't find a tenant until the 15th. Now you've qualified the tenant and are ready to have them sign a rental agreement. They are willing to sign and give you a check for all money they owe. However, they can't move in until the 1st and want the rent to start as of then.

If you allow the rent to start on the 1st, you will have lost another two weeks of income. I always tell the tenant that the property is now available and I can't lose two weeks rent waiting for them. They can move in on the 1st if they choose, but the rent must start on the 15th.

Usually what happens is that there's a discussion and the tenant will come back with an offer to compromise. What about splitting the difference—the rent can start one week before the 1st? I lose a week and they lose one as well.

If it's a strong tenant in a weak market, I'm willing to compromise. After all, it could take me another two weeks to find another suitable applicant.

What I usually do is counteroffer the following. The first month's rent will start one week before the 1st of the month. However, the following month, the tenant will pay five weeks' rent instead of four. That will move their payment date up to the 1st.

As noted earlier, it's always to your advantage to have the payment date on the 1st. Tenants will almost always agree to this compromise and be satisfied with it. If they don't agree, you can either go through the inconvenience of collecting rent at an odd time, which could cause significant difficulties later on when they move out and you want to rerent, or look for another tenant. I usually look for another tenant.

Leases and Losses—A Good Rental Agreement

Most people would concede that the most important document in landlord-tenant relations is the rental agreement. It spells out in writing just what that relationship actually is (subject, of course, to local, state, and federal laws). Armed with a strong rental agreement, you will have a much easier time dealing with your tenants. For one thing, they will know exactly what you expect. For another, if push comes to shove and you end up in small claims court, a good agreement will help you to prevail.

Many companies publish rental agreements and sell them in stationery stores, book stores that have real estate sections, and sometimes even through REALTOR® boards. Some state departments of real estate also have suggested forms, as do real estate agents. Of course, you could always go to a lawyer and have one drawn up from scratch specifically for your own needs.

After you've looked at a lot of different rental agreements, you'll begin to see that they all deal with the same information and potential problems. Most property managers I know start out with a published form and then add to it, adapting it to their own needs. This usually works very well for them.

COLLECTING THE DEPOSIT

One of the most important functions of the rental agreement will be to spell out the amount and the purpose of any deposit(s) you collect from

L A N D L O R D ' S   C A U T I O N

The rental agreement discussed in this chapter and found in the appendix works for me, but it may not work for you. Keep in mind that real estate laws are different from state to state and even within local areas. As a result, just because a form works in one area does not mean it is appropriate everywhere. It may not be suitable for your area. It may even contain clauses that are illegal or unenforceable in your state or locale. Or the wording may not be acceptable to a court in your area.

Therefore, my suggestion is that you do *not* use any forms unless you first take them to your own attorney to have them adapted to your specific locale and usage. That might cost you a few bucks, but it could save you a lot of money down the road. And the cost will be spread out over the years that you're a landlord.

the tenant. Before looking more closely at tenancy agreements, therefore, let's consider the deposit.

Deposits are typically collected at the time the tenant signs the rental agreement and pays the first (and last) month's rent. Sometimes a tenant may not have all the money to pay both the deposit(s) and the rent. There is nothing wrong with having the tenant pay the first month's rent upon signing the rental agreement with the written understanding that the deposit(s) are to be paid in full when the tenant moves in (which could be several days or even weeks later). However, it is vitally important to *not* let the tenant move in until the deposits are paid in full.

Any landlord who allows a tenant to move in—or even just begin moving belongings into the rental unit—without first having collected all monies up front is just asking for trouble. The tenant might never pay you another cent and you'd have to go through eviction without the benefit of having deposits to help ease the burden.

Always Give a Receipt

You'll need a receipt book that creates a copy every time you write a receipt. Every time you receive a deposit from a tenant, always give back a copy of the receipt, keeping the original for yourself. The receipt should state not only the obvious things such as name, date, and amount of the deposit, but its purpose and under what conditions it will be kept or returned. Never accept a check as a deposit without giving a signed receipt. It's not good business practice.

HOW BIG A DEPOSIT SHOULD YOU GET?

The obvious answer here is, as big as you can get. However, there are limitations. Tenants will balk at outrageously large deposits; they'll rent from someone else if you charge too much. Also, many states limit the size of the deposit you can take. (Check with your state or local department of real estate or housing.) For example, the cleaning/security deposit may be limited to one-and-a-half month's rent. (One way you may be able to get around this limitation is to accept several deposits for different purposes—for example, a cleaning/security deposit and then a separate deposit for a pet. Check with an experienced and knowledgeable property manager in your area.)

L A N D L O R D ' S   S T O R Y

Sally had a small two-bedroom house she was renting out. The market was bad, with too many rentals available for too few tenants. Her place had been empty for almost two months and she was getting desperate. She was ready to accept the first person who wanted to rent her unit, and she did.

The new tenants seemed okay, a credit check showed some problems but nothing catastrophic, but she couldn't verify their previous rental history because they were from out of the area and said they had always owned their own home before.

The biggest problem was the new tenants couldn't come up with all the rent money and deposits. But they wanted to move in immediately, on the 15th of the month. They said they would pay two weeks' rent in cash. Then, on the 1st, they would pay a full month's rent plus a large cleaning/security deposit. Sally accepted and they moved in.

But, on the 1st they said that jobs they were expecting to get didn't pan out. They didn't have any money. They were sorry and would move as soon as they could. The soonest they could move turned out to be six weeks later, just as Sally was halfway through eviction proceedings. She not only lost several months' rent (including clean-up time), plus costs, she also had no deposit to pay for the cleanup of the mess the tenants left.

The moral here is that you shouldn't jump from the frying pan into the fire. Having no tenant is better than having a bad tenant.

In some locales you may have to pay interest on deposits. Your state or local real estate or housing department will have this information.

Now that we have a handle on the deposit, let's consider the rental agreement.

RENTAL AGREEMENTS: MONTH-TO-MONTH VERSUS LEASE

The two basic types of rental agreements are month-to-month tenancy or a lease. (Actually the two types technically used are oral and written, but these days a landlord would be a fool, in my opinion, to use anything but a written agreement.) There are proponents of both month-to-month and longer-term leases. Keep in mind that the type you choose will have important ramifications on your relationships with your tenants.

The basic difference between the two types of rental agreements is that month-to-month is for an *indeterminate* period of time. Once begun, the agreement typically continues in force until cancelled, usually by 30 days' notice from either party. The lease, on the other hand, is for a specific period—usually one year, sometimes longer or shorter.

Most new landlords immediately seize upon the lease as the best document to use. They reason that it ties up the tenant for a specific period of time, so that the landlord presumably doesn't have to worry about re-renting the property. They anticipate signing the lease and then forgetting about it.

Unfortunately, that's not always the way it works out.

WHAT ARE THE CONCERNS WITH LEASES?

Property managers express a number of concerns with leases. These may lead them back to month-to-month tenancy as not wonderful, but preferable. Let's look at some of these concerns.

Inability to Raise Rents

Not only does the lease lock in the tenants for a specific period of time, but it also locks in the landlord. For example, if during the lease period the market tightens up and you discover that rentals similar to yours have increased $50 to $100 in rates, you can't increase your rates, short of breaking the lease. The lease specifies not only the amount to be paid each month but the total amount to be paid over the life of the lease. You're locked in. This is particularly worrisome with leases running a year or more.

Further, if during the term of the lease you decide to sell the property, you can't kick the tenants out so the new owner can move in. The tenants have tenancy rights to the property until the last day of the lease. In order to get them to agree to move out, you might have to offer some inducement, such as giving them six months' worth of rent. You're the one who is locked in.

But, of course, new landlords will point out that the tenants are locked in as well. Technically that's true, but for practical purposes, the tenants are only locked in to the degree that they want to be.

Are Tenants Really Locked In?

Let's say you have a two-year lease with a tenant for a house and after three months the tenant loses her job and can't work. She may very well be able to break the lease on the grounds that she no longer has the income to pay the rent. She may be able to get out of the lease and, essentially, owe you nothing for the remainder.

Maybe a tenant entered military service during the term of the lease. That could be sufficient grounds for breaking it.

Further, what if tenants don't have a good reason for breaking the lease, but simply up and move out? What are you going to do then? Usually your only recourse is to sue for the rent, usually as it comes due. The problem is that the tenants may be hard to find. They may leave the city or even the state, and tracking them down can be costly. Further, even if you find them, they may be "judgment-proof" or they may have no assets that you can easily attach.

You Must Mitigate Damages

Finally, you have a duty to mitigate damages. That is, you have a responsibility to try to rerent the property while you're out there trying to track down the tenants. This is not only a legal, but a logical thing to do. After all, why leave the property vacant when it can be producing rent? The problem is that the money you receive in rent must normally be subtracted from the amount you can claim from your tenant who moved out.

In short, what usually happens when a tenant skips on a lease is that the landlord quickly rerents the property and then turns the matter over to a collection agency, hoping that sometime in the future he or she may get some money back. As often as not, nothing comes in.

Breaking the Lease

On the other hand, let's say that you want to break the lease and get the tenant out and the tenant is unwilling. Your recourse may be to go to court. In a situation like that you had better have an iron-clad reason for wanting the tenant out and an attorney as good as Perry Mason.

SELLING A PROPERTY WITH A LEASE ATTACHED

You can sell your property even if you have leased it out, but the new owner takes over subject to the terms of the lease. That is, the new owner inherits the old tenant and the old lease. The biggest problem here usually involves the cleaning/security deposit. The new owner is probably responsible for paying it back when the tenant moves out (assuming the property is left clean). But, the old owner may keep the money, unless a provision for it to be transferred over is specified as part of the sale. In fact, as noted in Chapter 17, handling the cleaning/security deposit money is one of the more important elements in the sale of a property with a lease on it.

A Lease May Preclude Getting a Cleaning/Security Deposit

Finally, the one practical reason that property managers cite the most for not wanting to use a lease is that it may preclude your ability to get a substantial cleaning/security deposit. The reasoning here is really quite simple.

In a lease the landlord typically asks for first and last month's rent. Let's say you're renting a property for $750 a month. Double that (first and last month's rent) and the tenant now must come up with $1,500 in rent money before moving in. True, what you're asking is nothing more than paying the last month's rent first—when that last month rolls around, the tenant won't have to pay anything. But do you know anyone these days who has a lot of cash sitting around unused?

Now, add on top of this a cleaning deposit, which might be another $700 or so, and the move-in costs rise to $2,200. In a tight rental market, where there are loads of tenants and few properties, you might get this. But, in a market where landlords are in competition for a limited supply of tenants, you probably won't. Before coming up with all that money for you, a tenant is more likely to go to your competitor who charges less.

As a result, most landlords who insist on a lease end up getting a small or no cleaning/security deposit. They may, for example, accept only a couple of hundred dollars as the deposit.

The mistake that these landlords are making, in my opinion, is to think that the last month's rent is better than the cleaning/security deposit. Remember, you can't apply the last month's rent to cleaning. You can only apply it to rent. But the cleaning/security deposit can be applied either to rent or to cleaning. (See below for leases without the last month's rent and a larger deposit.)

WHEN THE LEASE EXPIRES

Many landlords fail to realize that in most states, when a lease expires (the time period runs out), the tenant does not automatically have to move. Rather, the tenancy converts to month-to-month and can stay that way indefinitely. To get the tenant out, you must now give notice, usually 30 days. The same applies to the tenants when they want to leave.

Note: Most state laws governing notice in month-to-month tenancy specify 30 days as a *minimum*. But, there is no maximum. Sometimes, if there's a need, I have agreed to 60 or even 90 days' notice. Tenants might insist on this, for example, if you're planning to sell the property. They want to be sure they have time to find a new rental if you sell and ask them to leave.

L A N D L O R D ' S   S T O R Y

Sally purchased a mountain rental home and found tenants who were willing to rent it for $750 a month. The tenants, however, were quite savvy and insisted on a lease offering Sally first and last month's rent plus a $100 cleaning deposit. Sally accepted the offer because the property was several hours by car from where she lived and showing it was a real hassle.

The tenants stayed the entire fifteen-month lease period and never called once to complain about anything. Their rent was also paid on time and Sally thanked her lucky stars that she had been so fortunate.

When she came to get the key from the tenants on the day they were to move out, she found they had already left, and had trashed her mountain home. Apparently they had used the property for a long series of parties during which the walls had received stains and holes in them, one toilet had been ripped from the floor and broken, a small fire had taken out part of the kitchen and roof and the grounds had been left to go to weed.

Yes, she had the $100 deposit, which the tenants didn't even try to claim, but they had done thousands in damage, most of which her insurance wouldn't cover. She also lost several months' rent while getting the property restored.

There are three morals here: (1) always get as big a cleaning/security deposit as possible, (2) always check up regularly on your rentals, even if you don't hear complaints from your tenants, and (3) never buy a rental far from your home.

HANGING YOUR HAT ON A MONTH-TO-MONTH TENANCY

As indicated, the most popular alternative to the lease is the month-to-month tenancy. This leaves both the landlord and the tenant free to pull the plug upon proper notification. If you want the tenant out, you simply give notice. On the other hand, if the tenants want out, they just give you notice and move.

The Revolving Door Tenancy

The biggest problem with the month-to-month tenancy, however, is the very indeterminacy of it. Most landlords don't want tenants moving in and out as though through a revolving door. No matter how big a deposit or how clean the tenants leave the property, there's always going to be some clean-up work after each tenant that you will have to do yourself and pay for yourself. Plus there's the time to rerent, anywhere from a few days to a month or more, during which you lose rent.

A landlord who has one tenant who stays for a year is usually doing far better than a landlord who has three tenants who stay for four months each. Unless you're running a motel/hotel, the last thing you want are itinerant tenants.

Incentives to Stay

Several landlords I know build a kind of incentive into their month-to-month agreements, hoping to get tenants to stay longer. They ask for a somewhat lower cleaning/security deposit and in addition ask for a non-refundable, one time cleaning fee (where allowed by local statute). Typically this fee is around $125. The tenant pays it up front and realizes that it is not going to come back.

However, the landlord then notes that for each month the tenant stays in the property, a portion of the fee will be refunded, perhaps $15 a month. If the tenant stays for nine months, the tenant gets back the full $125.

It's not a huge amount of money. But it is something that sticks in the tenants' minds. When they think about moving, they are reminded of it and it might be just enough to keep them staying put.

Hint: You want to be careful that the refund noted above doesn't constitute payment for work or you might be considered an employer under federal and/or state laws. If you're an employer, many rules and regulations may apply including withholding taxes, paying social security and workers' compensation, and more. Check with a knowledgeable property manager or an attorney in your area.

IT ISN'T NECESSARY TO REQUIRE THE LAST MONTH'S RENT ON A LEASE

You don't have to insist on the last month's rent in a lease. It can be a lease in every way including a start and end date and a listing of all money to be paid. It just doesn't have to specify a last month's rent paid up front. You still get the first month's rent and, usually, a larger cleaning deposit (which answers the problem noted earlier of a small deposit with a lease).

The advantage is that it is for a specific period of time. At least for its psychological advantage, the tenants are made aware that they are expected to stick around for the lease's term, perhaps a year or more.

The downside is that in forgoing the last month's rent, you lose the only real leverage you have with the lease. If the tenant walks, there's no cushion of a month's rent to ease the blow.

SHOULD YOU ASK FOR ATTORNEY'S FEES?

Rental agreements used to include a section that said that if a landlord and a tenant went to court over enforcement or other provisions of the agreement, the loser would pay the winner's attorney fees.

The reason behind this clause was two-fold. First, it put the tenants on notice that filing frivolous lawsuits against the landlord was going to be costly. Second, it gave the landlord at least the possibility of collecting the attorney's costs after winning the suit.

What If the Landlord Loses?

It used to be a forgone conclusion that, unless there were some unusual circumstances, by the time a tenancy suit got to court, the landlord was going to win. Not any longer. Today, as noted elsewhere, small claims courts may actually favor the tenant. Even if you feel you are 100 percent right, you have no guarantee that you are going to win. (Check out the movie "Pacific Heights" to get some idea of how bad things can go.)

Consider the consequences of losing:

- You're out your rent.
- You're out your attorney's fees.
- You're probably out cleaning costs.
- And now you're going to have to pay the tenant's attorney's fees!

As a result, today many landlords think twice before including a clause on the winner paying the loser's attorney fees. It's one of those apparently great ideas that could come back to haunt you.

ARBITRATION CLAUSES

Some landlords now insert binding arbitration clauses in their leases. If there is a dispute, both parties agree to take it before an arbitrator and agree to abide by the decision.

The trouble is that arbitrators who are specialists and belong to national arbitration associations often charge high fees. Thus, the cost of the arbitrator could be more than the amount in dispute. And getting both landlord and tenant to agree to some other third party as an arbitrator can be difficult.

AVOID UNENFORCEABLE CLAUSES

A rental agreement is a contract presumably binding on both parties. But even so, you cannot give up rights that you have under law by signing a contract. For example, you might want to have a clause in your rental agreement that precludes tenants from suing you for injuries they sustained while renting your property. The problem is that it's very hard to preclude someone from suing you. They usually have the right to sue just as they have the right to free speech.

Including unenforceable clauses only confuses and clutters up your rental agreement. Besides, they may give the other side more ammunition if push comes to shove and you end up in court.

Avoid legalese in your rental forms, even if you're a lawyer. Make it plain so it can be understood. You don't want your tenants to say they can't understand what they are signing.

RENTAL AGREEMENT

CAVEAT *Portions of the following rental agreement may not apply to your circumstances or may not be legal in your state or area. Do not use it as it is. Take it to a competent attorney in your area so that it may be customized for your state and locale and for your particular needs. The author and publisher assume no responsibility for the legality, appropriateness, or timeliness of this agreement.*

TENANCY AGREEMENT
MONTH-TO-MONTH/LEASE

THIS DOCUMENT IS INTENDED TO BE A LEGALLY BINDING AGREEMENT. READ IT CAREFULLY

City _____

State _____

Date _____

_____ (hereinafter referred to as Landlord) agrees to rent to _____ (hereinafter referred to as tenants) _____ the property described as _____ (hereinafter referred to as the premises), together with the following personal property: carpets, window coverings, light fixtures, built-in appliances, plus the following furniture:

_____

_____

Cross out and initial one of the two following paragraphs that do not apply and fill out and initial the one that does.

☐ **LEASE** This tenancy shall commence on this ___ day of _____, ____ and terminate on (date, month, year). The total rent for this lease period is $_____. The tenants shall pay first and last month's rent in advance. Upon expiration of this agreement, the tenancy shall revert to a month-to-month tenancy at $_____ per month.

☐ **MONTH-TO-MONTH** This tenancy shall commence on (date, month, year) and may be terminated by either party by giving a 30 day WRITTEN notice of termination to the other party.

1. RENT The rent is $_____ per month payable in advance on the ____day of each calendar month. Tenants to pay rent at the office of the landlord at _____ City_____ State_____ Zip_____ or at such other place as the landlord may from time to time designate.

2. BAD CHECKS Tenants shall pay a $_____ charge for handling of each check returned by the tenants' bank for "insufficient funds" or because the account is closed. Any dishonored check shall be treated as unpaid rent. It is hereby mutually agreed that if the tenants' bank returns two checks for whatever reason, thereafter tenants shall pay all rent in the form of cash, cashier's check, or money order. Any rent not received by the fifth day after it is due shall be paid only in the form of cash, cashier's check, or money order.

3. SECURITY DEPOSIT

UNDER NO CIRCUMSTANCES SHALL THE SECURITY DEPOSIT BE USED AS THE LAST MONTH'S RENT

Tenants agree to pay a refundable security deposit of $_____ before occupying the premises. Said deposit shall be refunded within ____days along with a written accounting of disposition of said deposit after tenants completely vacate the premises provided:

A: No damage, other than normal wear and tear, has been done to the premises, the furniture, or other personal property.

C. Premises are left clean. Landlord may deduct a portion of deposit to pay for certain cleaning if premises are not left clean.

D. All utilities that are the tenants' responsibility have been paid for in full and utilities have been properly notified of the tenants' departure.

E. All keys have been returned to the landlord.

F. All other conditions and terms of this agreement have been satisfactorily fulfilled.

The landlord may use all or a portion of this security deposit as may be reasonably necessary to

A. remedy tenants' defaults in payment of rent.

B. clean premises if left uncleaned by tenants.

C. repair damages caused by tenants to premises.

If any portion of the security deposit is used during the term of the tenancy to cure a default in rent or to repair damages, tenants agree to reinstate security deposit to its full amount within _____ days of written notice delivered to tenants by landlord in person or by mail.

In addition to the above, tenants also agree to pay a refundable pet security deposit of $_____.

In addition to the above, tenants also agree to pay a refundable waterbed deposit of $_____.

In addition to the above, tenants also agree to pay a NONREFUNDABLE cleaning fee of $_____.

4. LATE FEE It is hereby agreed that if the rent is not paid by the date it is due, tenants shall pay a late fee of $_____ for each day from the rental due date until the rent is paid.

5. INSPECTION Prior to taking occupancy, tenants agree to inspect the premises and any personal property therein, and to execute an inspection sheet which shall become a part of this agreement.

6. ACCESS Tenants shall allow the landlord access to the premises at reasonable times and upon reasonable notice for the purposes of inspection, making necessary repairs, or showing the premises to prospective tenants or purchasers.

7. NOTICE If rent is not paid by the due date, landlord may serve tenants with a ____ day notice to pay rent. If landlord agrees to accept payment of rent in full and late fees after servicing notice, tenants shall in addition be subject to a $_____ fee for preparing and serving the notice.

8. OCCUPANCY The total number of adults who may occupy the premises is _____. The total number of children who may occupy the premises is _____. Their names and birthdays are:

_____

_____

_____

No pet (except an animal trained to serve the handicapped such as a seeing eye dog) shall be kept on the premises without the specific written permission of the owner. The following pet(s) may be kept. _____.

9. VEHICLES Landlord shall provide ____ covered and ____ uncovered parking areas for tenants. Tenants shall keep a maximum of ____ vehicles on the premises. All tenants' vehicles not kept in designated locations must be parked in public areas. Tenants shall park no boat, trailer, or recreational vehicle on the premises continuously for more than ____ days without prior written approval of the landlord.

10. DAMAGES AND REPAIRS Tenants agree to pay for all damages to the premises done by the tenants or their invitees. Tenants agree not to paint, paper, alter, redecorate or make repairs to the dwelling, except as provided by law, without first obtaining the landlord's specific written permission.

Landlord agrees to undertake as soon as possible any and all repairs necessary to make the premises habitable and to correct any defects which are hazardous to the health and safety of the occupants, upon notification by tenants of the problem. If the landlord cannot reasonably complete such repairs within three days, he (she) shall keep tenants informed of the work progress.

All requests by tenants for service and repairs, except in the case of an emergency, are to be in the form of writing. Tenants agree to keep the premises in good order and condition and to pay for any repairs caused by their negligence or misuse or that of their family or invitees.

It is mutually agreed that it is the tenants' responsibility to repair certain items, such as windows broken or damaged subsequent to tenants' occupancy, at tenants' expense. If tenants are unable or unwilling to repair broken or damaged windows within a reasonable period of time, landlord may make such repairs and charge tenants. The cost of the repairs must not exceed the lowest bid by a competent worker.

As of occupancy, landlord warrants that all plumbing drainage is in good working condition. Tenants thereafter agree to pay for removing all stoppages caused for any reason except for roots, defective plumbing, backup from main lines, or undefined causes as determined by the plumber who clears the line.

11. USE The premises are to be used only as a residence. No commercial use is allowed. The tenants shall have the right to quiet enjoyment of the premises. The tenants agree not to disturb, annoy, endanger, or inconvenience neighbors nor use the premises for any immoral or unlawful purpose, nor violate any law ordinance nor commit waste or nuisance upon or about the premises. No waterbed may be used on the premises without the prior written consent of the landlord.

12. UTILITIES Landlord shall pay for the following utilities _____
_____ Tenants shall be responsible for opening, closing, and
paying all costs for the following utilities_____
If the tenants are responsible for trash, the tenants shall obtain and maintain trash and
garbage service from the appropriate utility company.

13. YARD MAINTENANCE Landlord shall be responsible for maintaining all common areas. Tenants shall be responsible for maintaining _____.
With regard to areas tenants are to maintain, they shall be kept clear of rubbish and
weeds. Lawns, shrubs, and surrounding grounds shall be kept in reasonably good condition. In the event tenants do not maintain premises in reasonably good condition,
landlord at his option may provide gardening service at \$_____ per month to be paid
for by tenants. Landlord shall be responsible for installation, repair, and replacement of
all below-ground sprinkler systems.

14. INSURANCE The landlord shall obtain fire insurance to cover the premises. Tenants are aware that landlord's insurance does not cover tenants' personal property and
they are encouraged to secure a tenants' insurance policy.

In the event of a fire or casualty damage caused by tenants, they shall be responsible for payment of rent and for repairs to correct the damage. If a portion of the premises should become uninhabitable due to fire or casualty damage due to no fault of the
tenants, they shall not be responsible for payment of rent for that portion. Should the
entire premises be uninhabitable due to no fault of the tenants, no rent shall be due until
premises shall be made habitable again. The landlord shall reserve the right to determine whether premises or a portion thereof is uninhabitable.

15. HAZARDOUS MATERIALS Tenants agree not to keep or use on the premises
any materials which an insurance company may deem hazardous or to conduct any activity which increases the rate of insurance for the landlord.

16. NEGLIGENCE Tenants agree to hold the landlord harmless from claims of loss
or damage to property and injury or death to persons caused by the negligence or intentional acts of the tenants or their invitees.

17. EMERGENCIES In the event of an emergency involving the premises, such as a
plumbing stoppage, the tenants shall immediately call the landlord at _____
or other phone number as the landlord may from time to time designate, and report
problem. In an emergency the landlord may enter the property without notice.

18. DELAY If the landlord shall be unable to give possession of the premises on the
day of the commencement of this agreement by reason of the holding over of any prior
occupant of the premises or for any other reasons beyond the control of the landlord,
then tenants' obligations to pay the rent and other charges in this agreement shall not
commence until possession of the premises is given or is available to tenants. Tenants
agree to accept such abatement of rent as liquidated damages in full satisfaction of the
failure of landlord to give possession of said premises on agreed date and further agrees

that landlord shall not be held liable for any damages tenants may suffer as a consequence of not receiving timely possession. If such delay exceeds _____ days from the commencement date, this agreement shall be considered void.

19. SUBLETTING Tenants shall not sublet, assign, or transfer all or part of the premises without the prior written consent of the landlord.

20. RULES Tenants shall comply with all covenants, conditions, and restrictions that apply to the premises. The tenants shall comply with all rules of a homeowner's association that apply to the premises.

21. ATTORNEY'S FEES If either party brings action to enforce any terms of this agreement or recover the possession of the premises, the prevailing party shall/shall not (cross out wording not desired and initial change) be entitled to recover from the other party his costs and attorney fees.

22. RESPONSIBILITY TO PAY RENT All undersigned tenants are jointly and severally (together and separately) liable for all rents incurred during the term of this agreement. (Every member is equally responsible for the payment of the rent.) Each tenant who signs this agreement authorizes and agrees to be the agent of all other occupants of the premises and agrees to accept, on behalf of the other occupants, service of notices and summons relating to tenancy.

23. SUBSTITUTION OF TENANTS In the event one tenant moves out and is substituted by another, the new tenant shall fill out an application and tenancy shall be subject to the approval of the landlord. No portion of the cleaning deposit will be refunded until the property is completely vacated.

24. HOLD OVER If after the date of termination of tenancy, tenants are still in possession of premises, they will be considered holding over and agree to pay rental damages at the rate of 1/30th of their then-current monthly rent per day of hold over.

25. OTHER CONDITIONS Each provision herein containing words used in the singular shall include the plural where the context requires. If any item in this agreement is found to be contrary to federal, state, or local law, it shall be considered null and void and shall not affect the validity of any other item in the agreement. The waiver of any breach of any of the terms and conditions of this lease shall not constitute a continuing waiver or a subsequent breach of any of the terms or conditions herein. The foregoing constitutes the entire agreement between the parties and may be nullified or changed only in writing and signed by both parties. Both parties have executed this lease in duplicate and hereby acknowledge receipt of a copy on the day and year first shown above. Time is of the essence in this agreement.

TENANTS ACKNOWLEDGE RECEIPT OF THE FOLLOWING:
- ☐ Move-in inspection sheet
- ☐ Homeowner's rules and regulations
- ☐ Entry key

☐ Community pool key
☐ Remote garage door opener
☐ Security gate card #_____
☐ Lead paint notice
☐ Smoke detector in operating condition
☐ Door lock notice
☐ Laundry room key
☐ Other _____

Tenant_____
Tenant_____
Landlord_____
Landlord_____

CREATING YOUR RENTAL AGREEMENT

I have included my rental agreement here as well as in the appendix. As I noted before, this agreement has worked well for me. Before you use it, take it to your attorney to determine if it will work for you, to adapt it to the laws in your area, and to your specific needs.

Also, keep in mind that it should be considered a "work in progress." Existing laws and regulations are constantly changing and new ones are always coming on the books. As the specific needs of your property evolve and are discovered by you, be prepared to update this agreement to meet changing needs.

You may also want to consider *Lease Writer,* a software program and book from Nolo Press that helps you create your own lease clauses. It's available from 2-Law (800-526-5588).

CHAPTER 6

Dealing with Required Disclosures, Security, and Health and Safety

Many first-time landlords, as well as many who have been in the business for years, are oblivious to the new health and safety requirements across the country affecting rentals. Today, you not only are required to provide your tenant with a habitable home, you may also be required to take precautions to be sure that the home is a safe and healthy environment.

Of course, I don't think any landlord wants to feel responsible for a tenant getting sick or injured, let alone face the legal liabilities that such an event would involve. In this chapter we'll look at some of the health and safety requirements that you may have to comply with to rent property in your area.

LEAD DISCLOSURES

Lead has been known for many years to have serious health effects. That is why it has been banned from paint since 1978, as well as gasoline and other products. In 1992 the Secretary of the Department of Health and Human Services called lead the "number one environmental threat to the health of children in the United States."

In the home it is possible to be exposed to lead from breathing dust in the air, drinking water from lead-contaminated pipes, ingesting food containing lead dust, even from contaminated soil in the yard. Lead is an insidious toxin because its effects, though sometimes deadly, may take many months or even years to produce visible effects.

At high levels, lead can cause convulsions, coma, and death. At low levels it can adversely affect the blood system, kidneys, the central nervous system, and the brain. It can cause problems such as hyperactivity, muscle and joint pain, high blood pressure, and loss of hearing. Children and fetuses are particularly susceptible to lead poisoning because it is more easily absorbed into growing bodies. Also, children are more likely to get lead in their systems because they tend to frequently put their fingers in their mouths or lick or chew on areas such as door jambs or window sills covered with lead paint. A simple blood test can determine if a person's bloodstream has high levels of lead.

Lead in Paint

The greatest source of lead in the home comes from lead-based paints which were routinely used until they were banned in 1978. Today when this paint weathers and dries out, it often turns into dust which can then be inhaled or ingested. Additionally, lead paint on the outside of homes may chalk up and fall to the ground, where it contaminates the soil. Other sources of lead contamination come from attempting to remove lead paint by scraping, sanding, or open-flame burning.

Lead paint is most likely to be found in homes built prior to 1978 on

- window sills and door jambs.
- doors and door frames, railings and banisters.
- trim on the inside of the home.
- the exterior of the home.

Lead in Water

In addition there is also a potential threat from lead in the drinking water of some homes, particularly those built around the turn of the century. Even today a short lead pipe may be used to connect a home's water system to the public utility, thus allowing the introduction of the metal into the water system.

In newer homes, copper pipes have mostly replaced galvanized steel. However, until recently it was common practice to use lead solder to join the copper pipes together. It has only been within the past decade that lead solder has been banned from use in water pipes in many states. (It has been replaced by a silver solder that works just as well, but costs more.) In addition, so-called brass faucets and fittings can sometimes leach lead. Newer standards for these fittings have mandated that they be lead-free and many even advertise this fact on their boxes.

Lead Cannot Be Easily Removed

Lead-based paint, when in good condition, is not usually a hazard. (The exception is when small children chew on it.) However, when lead-based paint chips turn to chalk, crack or peel, they become a serious hazard. The dust or chips can well up in shifting air and be inhaled or settle on food and be ingested by tenants.

It stands to reason, therefore, that if you have a rental that was built prior to 1978, you would want to limit the lead exposure to tenants. However, doing so is not necessarily easy or inexpensive.

For one thing, it is not usually possible to tell just by looking if a paint contains lead (just being glossy does not mean it is lead-based). Only a special test can determine if there's lead in the paint. The test for a full single family home costs around $300. (Your state health department can usually suggest a private laboratory or a public agency which may be able to help you test for lead in paint.)

Lead removal requires an expert. You should never attempt to remove it from a rental yourself (unless you're fully qualified) or you may make the problem worse. Remember, scraping, sanding, or using an open-flame torch will release lead dust into the air so that it can be inhaled or ingested. Also, do not use a home vacuum cleaner to try to capture lead dust. The bag that holds the debris may not be able to retain the tiny lead dust particles and by vacuuming you may actually be spraying lead dust into the air.

Unfortunately, expert lead removal is very expensive, primarily because it requires qualified people to do it who must wear expensive protective gear during the removal. It is not uncommon for it to cost upwards of $10,000 to remove lead paint from a whole house! For a thousand square foot rental unit it could be $5,000 or more.

Removing lead from the water system is equally difficult and expensive. Testing to find out if you have it, however, is much simpler. While lead is colorless, odorless, and tasteless, water testing kits are available for only around $20 and a professional can do it for around $100.

The only real way to remove lead from the water system is to replumb. However, if faucets are allowed to flow for a minute or so, you will usually get rid of lead that has accumulated in water standing in the pipes.

What Should the Landlord Do about Lead?

First, if your rental unit was built after 1978, chances are you don't have a problem with lead paint. (Contractors were allowed to use up remaining stocks of lead-based paint, however, so some homes built in 1978 and 1979 may still have some lead paint in them.)

However, if your rental was built prior to 1978, chances are very good that you have some lead paint in it. What must you do about this?

The federal government now requires that you provide each tenant with a statement using specific language regarding lead in the property and a booklet describing the dangers of lead. A copy of the statement can be found at the end of this book and booklets on lead are readily available from real estate agents, escrow companies, and title companies. You can also call the National Lead Information Center at 800-424-LEAD for booklets.

What You Are Not Required to Do as a Landlord

As of this writing, you are *not* required to

- conduct any investigation to determine if there's lead-based paint in the rental.
- remove any lead-based paint which may be found in the rental.

Be sure you are quite clear on this. If your rental was built in 1978 or earlier, you must provide a written disclosure to each tenant telling whether or not you know if there's lead paint on the property. But, whether or not you know of it, you are not required to remove it. In essence, it is up to the tenant to decide whether or not to live in the property where there might be a potential lead hazard.

THE LANDLORD'S DILEMMA

If you suspect your property has lead paint, should you remove it? Remember that removal must be done by a professional and can be very expensive. Further, removing the lead paint adds no value to your property. Removal simply is an expense item.

Many landlords just decide to make sure that the paint on their older properties is in good condition. In particular they repaint walls; doors, door jambs, and window frames; and the exterior with a good latex paint and see to it that there is no chipping, chalking, or other deterioration.

Unfortunately, covering over lead-based paint is not recommended as a cure. The reason is that the lead remains in the old paint and can be released at any time, as when a small child chews on a window sill.

Therefore, the landlord of an older building is faced with a true dilemma. If you have lead-based paint, you may feel that you can't in good conscience keep it, yet you probably can't afford to remove it.

Keep in mind that at some time in the future, the federal government may change the rules and require testing and/or mandatory removal of all lead-based paint from older buildings.

For more information contact the EPA at 800-621-8431.

PROBLEMS WITH ASBESTOS

Asbestos is a mineral fiber that in the past was added to a variety of products to strengthen them and to provide heat insulation and fire resistance. You can't tell if something contains asbestos unless you look at it with a microscope.

According to the American Lung Association, breathing high levels of asbestos fibers can lead to an increased risk of lung cancer; mesothelioma, a cancer of the lining of the chest and the abdominal cavity; and asbestosis, in which the lungs become scarred with fibrous tissue. However, the American Lung Association goes on to point out that most people exposed to small amounts of asbestos, as we all are in our daily lives, do not develop these health problems.

The real danger with asbestos in a rental is that it might be disturbed. When it is, asbestos material may release large amounts of asbestos fibers, which can be inhaled into the lungs. The fibers can remain there for a long time, increasing the risk of disease. Unfortunately, asbestos material often crumbles easily if handled, or is released into the air if sawed, scraped, or sanded into a powder.

Does Your Rental Have Asbestos?

Asbestos has in the past been used extensively in a wide variety of products including roofing shingles, insulation in walls and attics, sprayed-on ceilings, joint compounds (prior to 1977 when it was banned for this usage), artificial ashes and embers sometimes used in gas-fired fireplaces and heaters, some vinyl floor titles, and heat protectors such as stove pads. It also has been extensively used in the form of blankets around ducts and heating systems (particularly in steam pipes) as a heat insulator. The only way to know for sure is to hire a professional to conduct tests.

Hint: Don't try testing for asbestos yourself. The act of breaking open material to obtain test samples may release asbestos into the environment, creating the problem you're trying to avoid.

What Should You Do If You Have Asbestos in a Rental?

As of this time, there are no federal disclosure rules for asbestos (although there may be some local or state rules). That means the federal government does not require you to investigate to find out if you have asbestos, to remove it, or to inform tenants of it.

Further, you may be better off simply not touching existing asbestos. According to the American Lung Association, if you think asbestos may be present, the best thing is to leave the asbestos material that is in good condition alone. Generally speaking, material in good condition will not release asbestos fibers. There is no danger unless fibers are released and inhaled into the lungs or ingested.

Of course, it is a good idea to regularly check material you suspect may contain asbestos. Don't touch it, but look for signs of wear or damage such as tears, abrasions, or water damage. Damaged material may release asbestos fibers. This is particularly true if you disturb it often by hitting, rubbing, or handling it, or if it is exposed to extreme vibration or air flow. Sometimes the best way to deal with slightly damaged material is to limit access to the area and not touch or disturb it. Again, check with local health, environmental, or other appropriate officials to find out proper handling and disposal procedures.

If you discover asbestos material that requires removal or encapsulation, be sure to have a professional do it. From a liability point of view, you will probably want to be sure there are no tenants in the property during the removal period.

In general, if you're aware of any asbestos that you think poses a health hazard, you will probably want to get an inspection by a trained professional and then, if a hazard is demonstrated to exist, have it removed or encapsulated. Unfortunately, as with lead, the cost is high and doing the work usually adds nothing to the value of the property.

What About Asbestos Ceilings?

Between 1950 and the late 1970s, it was common practice in many parts of the country to spray an "acoustical" material onto ceilings. This gave the ceiling a nice textured look and also, supposedly, had acoustical properties. Unfortunately, the spray often contained asbestos.

Generally speaking, these asbestos-sprayed ceilings, which remain in many properties to this day, do not pose much of a health hazard as long as they are not disturbed. Testing is required to determine if they are asbestos and removal is done by professionals who usually wet the asbestos material and then scrape it. Other methods involve encapsulating by spraying with a shellac and then painting. Be sure to check with a professional for advice on how to handle your problem.

For more information on asbestos, contact your local American Lung Association for copies of "Indoor Air Pollution Fact Sheet—Asbestos." The EPA also provides a booklet called "Guidance For Controlling Asbestos-Containing Materials In Buildings." Phone 800-621-8431 or look at www.epa.gov/epahome/publications.htm.

OTHER TOXICS IN RENTAL PROPERTY

There is a long list of other toxic materials which may be in your rental property. Some of the more hazardous include

- *Carbon monoxide* in the air from faulty heaters.
- *Formaldehyde* in wall paneling and insulation.
- *Radon gas* in the air supply, particularly in basements and lower floors.

As of this time I know of no federal regulations requiring investigation to determine if any of these problems exist, their removal, or disclosures to tenants. However, it is not inconceivable that regulations with regard to these may be passed. Here is a brief summary of each and the hazard involved.

Carbon Monoxide

Carbon monoxide is a colorless, odorless gas. While it is not toxic itself, when inhaled and absorbed into the bloodstream it impedes the flow of oxygen. Often the person affected will not even be aware of the poisoning and may look for other reasons for the symptoms, which may include headache, dizziness, and nausea. Death can result from poisoning.

Carbon monoxide is generated from burning many different types of fuels, particularly when there is inadequate oxygen in the burning process. Fuels include charcoal, heating oil, kerosene, natural gas, propane, and wood. The most common culprits are wood-burning stoves and some space heaters that use propane or kerosene. Old fireplaces and gas stoves also can often release carbon monoxide. Also, a furnace with a bad heat exchanger may release it into the air.

As a landlord, if you use such fuels to heat your rental unit(s) you may want to supply a carbon monoxide detector. These cost around $50 and can be quite effective. Some rural and mountain communities require their use. If carbon monoxide is detected, you want to immediately fix or replace the offending appliance because this can be a life-threatening situation.

Formaldehyde

Formaldehyde is a highly pungent-smelling, colorless gas. In sufficient concentrations (usually above .1 parts per million) it can cause burning sensations in the eyes and throat, difficulty in breathing, and nausea. It can even trigger attacks in people with asthma. According to the EPA, formaldehyde has also been shown to cause cancer in animals and represents a cancer risk in humans.

Formaldehyde is widely used in the manufacture of building materials and household products. It also can be found as a by-product of combustion. Typical sources of formaldehyde in the home include building materials, gas stoves, glues and paints, kerosene space heaters, and preservatives. Probably the most common source of formaldehyde in the home comes from pressed wood products such as plywood that use urea-formaldehyde resins in their adhesives. Other sources are particleboard (typically used as subflooring and shelving); plywood paneling, particularly when the wood is hardwood; and medium density fiberboard.

In 1985 the Department of Housing and Urban Development (HUD) began restricting the use of plywood and particleboard in the construction of prefabricated and mobile homes to certain specified formaldehyde emission limits. In the past, some of these homes had formaldehyde problems, primarily because most were relatively small, well-insulated and sealed, and the manufacturers had used large amounts of high-emitting pressed wood products.

If your rental has a formaldehyde problem, you probably can smell it yourself. Tenants may be more or less sensitive to it and may or may not complain about the odor. (The odor is like sulphur, only more acrid. If you took a high school biology class, you probably know the odor of formaldehyde.) If you can't smell it, you probably don't have a problem.

The easiest way to deal with a formaldehyde problem is removal. Replace the wood paneling or particle boards causing the problem. Also increase ventilation. Maintain constant heat and humidity levels—formaldehyde emissions can be increased by heat.

For further information on formaldehyde, you can call the EPA Toxic Substance Control Act (TSCA) assistance line at 202-554-1404.

Radon Gas

Radon is a naturally occurring gas that is a known cancer-causing agent. According to the Surgeon General, it is the second leading cause of lung cancer in the United States. Its effects, however, are not immediate, but long term. It may take many years of exposure to radon to produce health problems. Because radon is colorless, tasteless, and odorless, it is difficult to tell if one has been exposed.

Radon occurs naturally in the earth when uranium in soil, rocks, and water breaks down. The radon in the earth can migrate into a building because air pressure there is often lower than pressure in the soil. In effect, the house acts like a vacuum, drawing up gases—including radon—from the earth.

Many low-cost radon testing kits are available through the mail and from hardware stores. They generally sell for less than $50. (Be sure you buy a kit that states that it "Meets EPA Requirements" or the requirements that your state may impose.)

Testing itself is usually done at the lowest living levels of the house. If a test reveals radon, it is almost always possible to install equipment that will reduce it to acceptable levels. This usually involves the use of fans, blowers, and ducts to better ventilate the lower levels of the property. You can do the work yourself or hire it out. Check in the yellow pages of your phone book for specialists in "Radon Reduction." (These companies are always available in areas where radon is a problem.) It has been estimated that properly installed radon reduction systems can cut radon levels by up to 99 percent in the home. The cost of radon reduction systems varies from as little as $500 to $3,000 or more.

Should you as a landlord be concerned about radon? It is just one more hazard to watch out for. While federal rules don't require inspection, correction, or disclosure of radon as of this writing, the laws can change. However, in those areas of the country where there is a severe radon problem, local or state laws may be in effect. Check with a local real estate agent or building and safety department.

For more information on reducing radon, get a copy of the EPA's "Consumer's Guide to Radon Reduction" by calling 800-621-8431, or online at www.epa.gov/epahome/publications.htm.

DO YOU NEED A SMOKE ALARM?

Most areas of the country now require that at least one smoke alarm be present in all rental properties. In some cases there must be a smoke alarm in all bedroom areas as well as near the kitchen. If you don't have a smoke alarm in a rental and there's a fire, your liability could be enormous.

There's no reason not to use smoke alarms in rentals. They are inexpensive and tenants are usually grateful to have them.

There are at least two different kinds of smoke alarms. One uses a tiny bit of radioactive material in an ion chamber to detect smoke. These are better at detecting rapidly burning fires. A photocell type of detector also detects smoke and is better at sounding the alarm for low flame, smoldering fires. Detectors that contain both types are available for less than $50. Ion chamber detectors are readily available for less than $10.

When installing a smoke detector, be sure to check with your local building and safety department to find out whether your local code requires them to be battery operated or hard-wired into the property. Some areas require one type, other areas another. Often the code is very strictly enforced.

If you have an existing building that is not wired for a smoke detector and the code requires it, have an electrician run an electrical wire from a plug or hot ceiling outlet to a suitable place for the detector. This may cost $100 or more, but if the local code requires it, you do not have a choice.

If you use battery operated smoke detectors, be aware that the batteries are usually only good for about a year. It's an excellent idea to have a regular battery replacement schedule to follow. It also helps to write down the date the battery is installed on a small adhesive label and attach it right to the detector so you'll know how current the battery is.

Be sure you show tenants where the smoke detector(s) are located and how to test them. Also, let them know that if the detector starts chirping, it's not a cricket, but a sign that the battery is low and that they should let you know so it can be changed. For liability reasons, it's important to get a signed statement from the tenant that they have a working smoke alarm (see the appendix for a sample letter).

FIRE EXTINGUISHERS

A fire extinguisher provides a self-help way for a tenant to put out a small fire. Fires most often start in the kitchen, usually as the result of grease burning. Other common places for fires are the garage and any room with a fireplace or a space heater.

If you have an apartment building, the local building and safety department may require that you maintain a fire extinguisher of a certain weight (the weight being the fire retardant material it contains) in hall-ways and other areas (such as washrooms). You may be required to keep one extinguisher of a certain weight per so many units.

In single family to up to four-unit rental buildings requirements for extinguishers are often more lax. Sometimes you must call the local building and safety department to find out what the fire extinguisher requirements are for your type of rental.

If there's a fire, and you didn't provide an extinguisher when one was required, your liability will be enormous. Indeed, if someone is seriously injured or, God forbid, dies, you could face criminal prosecution!

I hope I've scared you enough to consider putting in fire extinguishers. They are relatively inexpensive (often costing under $20) and can pay for themselves in peace of mind alone.

Modern extinguishers are rated for different types of fires. "A" is for conventional fires fed by such things as cloth, rubbish, paper, and wood. "B" is for fires fed by grease, paint, oil, and flammable liquids. "C" is for electrical fires. A good extinguisher for a rental is usually one that has an ABC rating and is all-purpose.

In addition, there's the amount of fire retardant material in the extinguisher. The higher the number associated with a letter, the greater the amount of retardant and the bigger a fire it will cover. Most small fire extinguishers contain three to five pounds of retardant and are enough for a small fire. But this means they only last around ten seconds.

I always have at least one fire extinguisher in each rental unit. I also point out where the extinguisher is to the tenant and I have them sign a statement that they know its location (see the Appendix for sample statement). I also instruct them that if they ever have to use the extinguisher, to keep it at least five to six feet away from the flames. Otherwise the spray from the extinguisher could blow the flames to another location.

One final word about the charge in the extinguisher. Extinguishers only work if they are charged. The common and least expensive type, dry chemical, cannot be partially discharged. They only get one usage. Therefore, if you provide this type, you should check on a regular basis to see that they are charged. Also affix a label (which usually comes with the extinguisher) giving the last date it was checked.

Most extinguishers claim they can be recharged once used. The trouble is, it's usually only the factory that can do this and the cost for transporting them back and forth and charging them is usually more than the cost of a new extinguisher. It's better to think of them as disposable. However, be sure to instruct tenants not to "test" the extinguisher by trying it out, as that will discharge it. (Buy extinguishers that come with a gauge that shows if it's charged.)

POOL/SPA SAFETY

Many times rental units will have a pool, spa, or both. If your building has these, be aware of your increased liability. Pools and spas may be attractions to hook tenants, but they can also provide terrible complications if someone gets injured in them. Generally speaking there are four concerns regarding pools and spas: (1) safety at the location, (2) fencing, (3) insurance, and (4) maintenance.

Safety at the Location

Usually you must provide a set of pool and spa rules and safety precautions. They should be located where they can be seen and are easily read in the language(s) most commonly used by tenants. Rules include such things as who must not use the spa (young children, people with heart problems, etc.), how to revive someone who has drowned, and who to call in an emergency.

Be wary of limiting access to the pool, as it might be considered discrimination. For example, you may be able to say that no one can use the pool between 10 PM and 8 AM. But, you probably will not be able to say that supervised children are prohibited from using it. You may not even be able to say that children may not use the pool during certain hours. Reread Chapter 3 or contact HUD.

Fencing

You only want authorized people to use your pool (tenants). You also don't want children to wander into the pool area, accidentally fall in and drown. That means you do want to have your pool/spa completely fenced. This is also usually a building and safety code requirement.

Typically the fence must be at least five feet tall and must have a spring-loaded locking gate. Don't let the fence or gate deteriorate to the point where small children can sneak in. If you don't have proper fencing and someone gets into your pool, even if they are trespassing on your property, you could be in more hot water than you ever imagined possible.

Insurance

To cover your liability for having a pool/spa in a rental area you must carry extra liability insurance. Be sure that it specifically covers the pool/spa area. I maintain at least a $2 million liability policy, although many landlords feel that $3 million is minimal. Typically this coverage is obtained by getting an umbrella liability policy over the top of your regular insurance policy. Check with your insurance agent.

Maintenance

Spas and pools need maintenance. They must be regularly cleaned, the acid/base balance must be correctly adjusted, and there must be a cleansing agent such as chlorine used to inhibit the development of algae and diseases in the water. You don't want algae (yellow, brown or black) because it will ruin your pool. You don't want diseases in the water, because these could make your tenants ill. So you need to either maintain the pool properly yourself or hire a service to do it.

If I have a pool at a rental, I always explain proper usage to my tenants and have them sign a statement that they are aware of how the pool should be used and of the dangers inherent in it.

By the way, if you have a slide or diving board at the pool, my suggestion is to remove it. The chances of someone being injured while using either are enormous. I don't think it's worth the liability to keep them there.

WATER HEATER SAFETY

For those who live in earthquake country, (California and most of the West Coast, as well as other parts of the U.S.) as well as areas where hurricanes are common, there are certain safety precautions that must be taken. The most common involves strapping the water heater.

Water heaters are actually vertical containers of water. They are very heavy when full and normally very stable. However, when the house or earth moves they can sway from side to side and even topple over. When they do, they usually break their water lines as well as the electric or gas lines leading to them. They can cause water damage and fires.

To prevent this, local regulations often require water heaters to be strapped to walls so that they cannot sway in most earthquakes. Some communities require it of rental units. In any event, it's a precaution that's well worth taking by anyone who owns rental property.

The actual method of securing the water heater is usually spelled out in local or state codes. Check with a good local agent or your building and safety department for details.

I always have my tenants sign a statement that they are aware that the water heater has been strapped. (See end of book for statement.)

RAISING GAS APPLIANCES IN THE GARAGE

Many flammable gasses are heavier than air. This applies to propane, gasoline, and others.

In a rental, this means that in a garage, there could be gas fumes escaping from a car's gas tank lingering close to the ground. A person who is standing close might not detect them. However, a water heater, clothes dryer, or other appliance with a pilot light could set them off, causing an explosion.

That's why many local and state governments require any such appliances located in a garage to be at least 18 inches off the floor. Compliance usually means simply buying a wood platform (typically available for this purpose in local hardware stores) and raising the water heater or appliance onto it. The cost is often under $25.

The chances are that a gas explosion in the garage will never happen to your rental. But if it does and you didn't comply with local regulations, you could be held responsible.

SECURITY PEEPHOLES

Peepholes, also called peepscopes, are optical devices that are fit into doors so you can see who's on the other side without opening the door.

They are particularly useful in blind entrances. They are commonly found in multiple-unit rental buildings. While peepholes may not be required in your rental, they are a good idea, as they add safety to a property.

A peephole device typically costs under $10 and is simple to install (you just have to cut the hole to the correct size). I would get one that offers a wide-angle view to the person inside, but is blind to the person trying to look in from the outside.

SECURITY LOCKS

Change the locks or at least change the keying of the locks for each new tenant. Be sure that the locks securely hold the doors. Many landlords favor a double locking system—a regular door handle lock plus a deadbolt.

Some tenants have sued landlords for not providing secure premises because the locks were inadequate. You don't want this problem. (See also Chapter 8 for more on door locks.)

LIGHTING

It's important that you provide adequate lighting of common areas at night, particularly if it's a multiple-unit dwelling. There are two important reasons for this. The first is to prevent accidental falls. The last thing you want is a tenant to trip over something and claim that he or she couldn't see adequately because of poor lighting.

The second reason is safety. Bright lighting discourages criminal activity. You don't want crimes committed on or near your property.

Today bright lighting is inexpensive and easy to install. Super-bright halogen lights can illuminate the front, sides, and back of buildings with ease. (Be sure to also brightly illuminate parking areas.)

CHECKING OUT EMPLOYEES

As a landlord, particularly when you have a large complex of rental units, you will need to hire employees such as gardeners, maintenance help, and rental agents. Be sure that you do a thorough job of checking these people out, including a police records check (you should obtain their permission to do background checks). Some landlords insist all of their people be bonded and the bonding company itself requires a thorough check.

Remember, the people you hire will be in close contact with your tenants. They probably have access to the inside of the rental units by means of master keys. The last thing you want is an employee to attack or rob a tenant. A thorough check at the time you hire someone can be used as a defense that you did your best. Also, do repeat checks. If you discover an employee with a problem (such as thievery), get rid of him or her as fast as legally possible.

Cleaning Up and Preparing to Rent

Some landlords make the serious mistake of thinking that they're doing the tenants a favor by providing a rental. They figure it's up to the tenant to get the property into habitable shape. On the other hand, other landlords feel that the new tenants are like guests coming into their homes. They scrub and clean as if they were expecting their son's new bride to be spending the night.

Getting the property so that it will appeal to a prospective tenant is somewhere in between. In this chapter we'll consider what you can do, what you should do, and what you can forget about doing.

The moral here is that you have to do a good, thorough job of cleaning if you want to get a good tenant.

MUST DO

Perhaps the best way to primp up your property so that it will appeal to a prospective tenant is to separate those areas that you must work on from those that you can forget. Let's consider the "must do" areas first:

- *Entry.* Clean or repaint the front door. Be sure the door handle is clean and that the entryway is swept. Put a new floor mat down, if necessary.

  First impressions are critical. The first thing the prospective tenant sees is the entry; be sure it looks great. A new coat of paint on

L A N D L O R D ' S   S T O R Y

Our friend Hal had a house he was trying to rent. The last tenant had left it in a bit of a mess and Hal realized he couldn't rent it like it was. So he hired a service to come in and clean only the entrance hall, living room, and kitchen—those areas that prospective tenants first saw. The service did a reasonably good job and when tenants came in, they were suitably satisfied with the premises . . . until they went to the bathrooms, particularly the one off the master bedroom. There were bottles and creams spilled around, the sink had hairs in it, the toilet hadn't been cleaned—you get the idea. Needless to say the house stayed unrented until Hal finally called the service back to finish the job.

the front door only takes a few moments and it can make a world of difference.

- *Living room, dining room, hallways, and bedrooms.* Shampoo the carpet; polish the floors. Paint any walls that have marks on them (it only takes an hour or so per room with today's modern latex paints and washable equipment). Clean the windows and window coverings.

Hint: Do not try to *clean* walls. Unless it's a very superficial mark that can be removed by a gentle sweep of a sponge with household cleaner on it, you'll only succeed in digging into the paint and creating an obtrusive "hole." Even if you do get the area clean, chances are it will make the surrounding areas look dirtier by comparison.

Dust and clean blinds, closets (including shelves), window sills, and baseboards. Dry clean draperies.

- *Kitchen.* This is a vital area. If it's clean, prospective tenants will feel the whole house is clean (assuming you've haven't left a mess in the bathrooms like Hal).

Be sure to clean the oven(s) thoroughly, especially see-through windows. If you have an electric range, don't waste time cleaning the "spill catchers" under the heating units—replace them. They only cost a few dollars apiece and are readily available at most hardware or grocery stores. Don't forget to clean the stove hood.

Thoroughly clean the sink, dishwasher, and all other appliances. Be sure to wash down the walls (assuming they have washable *gloss* paint) and wash and wax the floors.

Be wary of any bad odors or lingering smells. Use a pine oil cleaner and air freshener to take care of this.

- *Baths.* Clean the tub/shower, sink, and toilet. Clean around the base of the toilet as well. Wash the walls (assuming they have washable *gloss* paint) and wash and wax the floors.

    As with the kitchen, use a pine oil cleaner and air freshener to eliminate bad odors or lingering smells.

If that seems like a lot, it is. Assuming that the tenant leaves the property relatively clean, you could still have a couple of good days of cleaning ahead of you. But remember, a clean house attracts a clean tenant.

Hire a Cleaning Service

You don't like cleaning? I don't blame you; neither do I. When I first started with rentals, I used to do the cleaning myself on all my rentals. However, in recent years I've found that it just doesn't pay. Usually for a hundred dollars or so, I can get a service to clean the entire unit far better than I can do it myself.

Worried about the extra cost? I build it into the monthly rental. I set aside $10 a month out of the rent for one year and then use the savings to hire the cleaning service. Even if I had to pay for it out of my pocket, it's worth it to me not to feel that I'm a maid to my tenants.

DON'T DO

There are also a number of things that you don't want to do because they waste time and money on work that isn't necessary:

- *Don't wash walls except in kitchen and baths.* Today, most residential rooms (with the exception of kitchen and bath) are painted with a *flat* latex paint. If you go to the store and check out a can, it almost always says, "washable." Don't believe it for a minute.

What happens is that over time walls get both uniformly dirty and marked in certain spots. When you look at a wall that hasn't been painted in a year or so, you will see the marks, scratches, stains, and so forth. But, you won't see the overall dirt. Because it's everywhere, it doesn't stand out.

But just try to wash down the marks or spots on a wall painted in flat latex and you'll see more dirt than when you started. What happens is that where you washed is clean, while everywhere else now looks especially dirty. The overall dirt shows up by comparison. (This isn't usually the case with kitchen/bath walls that are usually small and use high gloss paint. The dirt tends to uniformly come off these walls with just a sponge and mild detergent.)

So, unless you plan to carefully wash all bedroom, living, dining room, etc., walls, any washing at all will only make matters worse. That's why I never suggest washing—instead paint. Painting walls these days is cheap. (For bathrooms and kitchens, wash walls from floor to ceiling. Otherwise the water running through the dirt on the walls may leave marks that even painting won't cover!)

- *Don't overscrub.* I once hired a cleaning person who came in and was so determined to get the kitchen sink clean, that she actually scrubbed through the porcelain! You want the property to look clean, not operating-room sterile.

- *Don't install new when old will do.* There may be rust marks in the dishwasher tray. Replace the tray, not the dishwasher. The tiles in the sink may have a few cracks. Clean and regrout; don't replace them. The carpet has soiled areas and is worn in some walkways; shampoo and use cleaners. Consider a runner to cover the heavily walked on areas. The faucet leaks. Put in a new washer, not a new faucet.

  What you want to end up with is a property that's clean, tidy, serviceable, and profitable. Don't sink your profits in unnecessary repairs. Remember, the tenant is only renting it—not buying it.

- *Don't keep outmoded features.* In bathrooms, sinks are important. You can replace a stand-alone or wall hanging sink that looks old-fashioned and cheap with a modern cabinet and sink top for less than $250. It will make the bathroom look brighter and more modern, and will attract a better class of tenant.

An ancient chandelier hanging in the dining room can date the rental. A new, inexpensive one can modernize it.

Old, dark paneling can be depressing and steer potential tenants away. Modern light paneling or even painting over dark wood can make a big difference.

You get the idea. Many old-fashioned features can be quickly, easily, and inexpensively replaced or updated. Doing so will give your rental a much more appealing look.

WHO PAYS FOR THE COST OF RENTAL PREPARATION?

Many landlords look at their job as having two functions only: collecting rents and denying tenant complaints. They tend to see rental cleanup and preparation as an extra and as such, they don't see why they should have to pay for it. Their perspective is that either the tenant who moved out (and left the place dirty) or the tenant who's moving in (and wants the place clean) should pay for the cleanup.

The problem is that there's always going to be some cleanup work that can't be charged to the leaving tenant and some dirt that the new tenant won't tolerate. That cleanup is the responsibility of the landlord.

Carpets are perhaps the best example. Over the course of a tenancy, carpets are normally going to not only get some wear and tear, but are also going to accumulate dirt. It's not the tenant's fault. It happens. It happens even in your own home.

Should you ask the leaving tenant to pay for cleaning the carpet? I don't think so.

If you do, the tenant is very likely to say, "I'll clean it before I leave." (They do this to save the money it will cost them out of the deposit if you do it.) Then the tenant goes out to a local grocery store, rents a steamer, and essentially ruins your carpet. Yes, it might look superficially clean. But chances are the dirt has only been rubbed off the surface and deposited deeper in the pile. Often within a few weeks after the new tenant moves in the carpet is dirty again, and this time it's more difficult—and expensive—to clean.

I think it's better to just accept the fact that as a landlord, some costs must be borne with a tenant turnaround and carpet cleaning is one of them.

Other areas that are the landlord's responsibility include any repainting that's needed as well as the replacement of any fixtures that are outdated. (Of course, you can charge the departing tenant for damage to walls, paint, and fixtures.)

WHEN SHOULD I SHOW THE PROPERTY?

A great rule to remember is that tenants have no imagination. If they see a dirty property, they'll always think of it as dirty. Thus, if you show your rental *before* you clean it up, you could actually be driving away good tenants.

I prefer to wait until I have my rentals cleaned up before showing them. If someone absolutely has to see one, I will show it during the cleaning process. I always avoid showing it dirty.

Yes, this may lose me a few days of rental time. But, on the other hand, I usually end up with a better tenant who takes better care of the rental.

CHAPTER 8

Moving the New Tenant In

You've found tenants, checked out their qualifications, and signed a rental agreement, and now they're ready to move in. What will your relationship be?

If you do it right, you'll go a long ways toward having a successful landlord/tenant relationship. Do it wrong and you will be setting yourself up for more trouble than you can imagine.

GET THE MONEY FIRST

Before the tenants move in, you need to get the money for both the first (and last, if you require it) month's rent, plus all deposits. Preferably it will be in cash or a cashier's check. Practically speaking, however, most tenants will hand over a personal check. If you accept a personal check, run it over to *their* bank (at least this first time) and get it certified. This means that their bank certifies that the funds are available and puts a hold on them—it pretty much guarantees the funds to you. This may take you a few minutes, but it's well worth the time.

> **Hint:** Never let the tenant move in until you have the *cash*. After all, what if you take their personal check to their bank and find that they don't have sufficient funds to cover it and they're already in your property?

Once you're satisfied that the money is in hand, you're ready to help the tenants move in. Keep in mind that how you handle the move-in will set the tone for the tenancy and will have repercussions later on when they move out.

Caution: Sometimes after you and the tenants agree upon a move-in date, the tenants will want to move a few of their belongings into the property ahead of time. Although this sounds perfectly innocent, there can be all sorts of problems associated with it.

If the tenants move anything onto the property (particularly if you loan them a key to do this), you have, for practical purposes, given them possession. If for any reason you don't go through with renting to them (they don't come up with all the money, there is a problem with the walk-through, they decide to back out) you have the matter of getting their possessions out of the property. In the old days, you might have just taken their stuff and dumped it outside. Not anymore. Now, you might actually have to evict them to get it out!

I'm very firm when it comes to moving anything in early. The answer is *no*. In most cases the tenants can find a friend or relative who can store their things. In a worst case they can use a public storage facility.

MEETING THE NEW TENANTS AT THE PROPERTY

The time has come when you officially turn the property over to the tenants. This is usually set up as a combination event. You'll conduct a walk-through (described in detail in the next chapter), go over any special concerns, and hand them an *instruction sheet* explaining when and where to pay the rent, how to handle moving out, and so on, then hand them the keys. When you turn over the keys, it's their rental.

This is a very important meeting because it sets the tone for the tenancy. Plan on setting aside an hour or more for this meeting, for you have many things to accomplish.

WHAT ABOUT LOCKS AND KEYS?

After you've finished the walk-through and you've both signed off on the inspection sheets (described in detail in the next chapter), give the tenants keys to the property. Get a receipt for the keys. Incorporate a statement on the walk-through sheet that the tenants have received x number of keys; have the tenants sign it.

A word of caution should be made here regarding door locks. As the landlord, it is your responsibility to see that you are providing a property that can be properly secured. That means a reasonably safe door lock. Most locks that you buy in the store will fit this need. For added safety, you may also want to include both a deadbolt—particularly in rental units located in high-crime areas—and a peephole in the door to see who's on the other side without opening it.

One problem, however, arises if you indeed have a good lock system, but then hand over the keys to a new tenant *without changing the locks.* It's conceivable that the previous tenants could have made additional keys and retained them, unbeknownst to you. They could now use them to get back into the property during the occupancy by the new tenants, perhaps to rob them or do something worse.

Because it costs a fair amount of money to put all new locks into a property, one solution is to remove all of the locks and take them to a locksmith. There, for a relatively small amount of money, the locksmith can not only rekey them, but make sure one key fits both front and back entrances. This only works, however, if you have good quality locks to begin with. Cheap locks often can't be easily rekeyed.

I know one property manager who tries to save money by having the tenants sign a statement that they will not make additional keys. In addition, on each key he gives them he has stamped, "Do not duplicate." He claims that he's never had a problem with this system. To me, however, it seems chancy. The safe way is to change the locks.

Inform Tenants about the Rekeying

When I hand over the keys, I always make it a point to note that the locks have all been rekeyed. I then hand the tenants a copy of my receipt from the locksmith showing that the work was done. The tenants frequently say that it's okay, they don't need the receipt, but I insist they look at it. It establishes my credibility and demonstrates my concern for their security. I also have them sign a receipt for the keys.

LANDLORD'S STORY

This story is so bizarre, it's almost unbelievable. But I swear it is true.

When I first started in real estate, I had a property manager friend whose job was overseeing a large apartment development having hundreds of units. She received rents, took in deposits, and in the course of business, handed out keys to tenants. The owner had provided her with an elaborate set of keys—several for each unit—and she took great pains to be sure that each renter received the correct key.

One day when I had brought in a couple who wanted to rent a unit, a tenant came in to complain that his neighbor had gotten into his apartment and, he said, stolen some items. Naturally my property manager friend was quite upset and went to investigate. I went along, too.

It turned out that the owner had not bothered to have each lock separately keyed. Instead, there was only one master key, which opened all of the units. My friend had unknowingly handed out the master to each tenant! There had been no problem until one unscrupulous tenant had discovered the fact and had taken advantage of it.

My friend immediately accosted the owner and demanded an explanation. The owner laughed and said it had worked fine, until someone had discovered what he had done. "As long as nobody knows," he said, "what's the difference?!"

Needless to say, all the locks were rekeyed and the owner had to make good on the items taken. But that such a thing could happen is almost unbelievable. The moral, of course, is don't let your tenants find out the hard way that you haven't rekeyed the locks. Do it automatically every time you get a new tenant. (In some locales, rekeying is now a mandatory requirement of the law.) And don't use master keys.

WHAT TO GIVE AND TELL NEW TENANTS

When a new tenant moves in, I always give them a welcoming tour including a couple of "presents." Doing this saves me a lot of headaches down the road.

Plumber's Helper

In one of the bathrooms, usually under the sink, I indicate that I've given them a "plumber's helper." This is a plunger that can be used to unplug a toilet. I then proceed to show them how to use it.

A plumber's helper is almost a necessity in any home because toilets get plugged up for a variety of reasons. A tenant who has and uses a plumber's helper can save you the cost of a trip to the property by a plumber. (I also point out that the cost of unplugging clogged plumbing will be borne by me if the problem is damaged pipes or roots in the drain system, but by the tenants if it's caused by something—such as toys, sanitary napkins, hair brushes, or whatever—they've dropped down the drain.)

Allen Wrench

I also provide them with an Allen wrench that fits the garbage disposal, assuming the rental unit has one. The Allen wrench goes underneath and allows you to manually turn the garbage disposal, thus clearing it when it's clogged. I show the tenant how to use the wrench. A tenant who's good with an Allen wrench can save me lots of trips to the property.

Don't worry about the cost of the plumber's helper and the Allen wrench. Between them they are less than $5 and well worth the expense.

Warning: There could be some liability in providing the wrench and plumber's helper. Tenants could conceivably injure themselves attempting to fix a problem. If you're worried about this, then don't provide the tools. Instead bite the bullet and pay to have repair work done, or do it yourself.

How to Work the Appliances

I also go through and carefully explain how to use the various appliances. If the stove has a timer oven, I explain how to use it. I show them how to work the dishwasher. If the unit has a refrigerator, I explain how to set the temperature. Don't assume that tenants automatically know how to work all the appliances. Even if they know how to operate one brand of appliance, they may not know how to work the brand in your unit.

How to Operate the Sprinklers

If the rental unit has lawn sprinklers that are electrically controlled, I show them where the box is and explain that the sprinklers are set to water on certain days and hours. I ask them what hours they would prefer to have the sprinklers come on and then set them. I then ask the tenants not to change the watering settings without calling me first. There's two reasons for this. First, it's often difficult to set the timers for electric sprinklers and the tenants might inadvertently set them too often, too seldom or the wrong times. Second, if the tenants are paying for the water, there's a tendency for them to set the timers back so the lawns don't get enough water.

L A N D L O R D ' S   S T O R Y

Sally bought a 15-year-old home and rented it out to a couple without learning about the use of the appliances herself, or explaining them to the tenants. During Thanksgiving, she got an emergency call from them saying that the electric oven was broken. They had their Thanksgiving turkey inside and there was no heat.

Sally sympathized with them and let them cook their bird in her own oven. The next day she sent an electrician out to fix the problem. The electrician reported back, however, that there was no problem. The tenants had inadvertently set the timer on the oven. With it activated, the oven wouldn't go on until the designated hour, which happened to be at two in the morning. The only correction needed was to turn the timer off. He showed the tenants how to do that and they were mortified, but pleased. He also sent Sally a bill for $85.

This true story shows how important it is to completely familiarize yourself with your rental, as well as explain all of the features to your tenants.

Where Are the "Turn-Offs?"

It's also a good idea to walk around the property and show the tenants how to turn off the water, gas, and electricity. This is particularly important if there should be a water leak, a short in a fixture, or a fire on the property. After an earthquake, quickly turning off the gas can save your property from burning down.

It's important to inform the tenants that once the gas has been turned off, it must not be turned on again until the gas company comes by to do it. Turning off the gas may turn off pilot lights in appliances which must be individually lit once the gas is turned back on.

Where Are the Smoke Alarms?

I also show the tenants exactly where the smoke alarms are located and test each one to demonstrate that it's working. I point out the location of the fire extinguisher(s) and any other special features the unit may have, such as sprinklers in case of fire or a security alarm system. I also have them sign a statement that they've inspected the smoke alarms, fire extinguishers, etc., and they are in operating condition.

EXPLAIN ABOUT THE UTILITIES

It's a good idea to walk the tenants to where the garbage is kept if it's an apartment building and explain about not overfilling any dumpsters. If it's a single family unit, explain what day the garbage is collected, how many cans are allowed, if recyclables are to be separated, and where they are expected to place their cans.

I provide a list of the phone numbers of all the utility companies. That makes it a lot easier for the tenants to get the utilities turned on. The list also provides some other service information. Most of the information is readily available in the phone book, but presenting it to the tenant on a sheet they can keep handy is useful to them, and makes a good impression.

WISHING THE NEW TENANTS WELL

Finally, I wish the new tenants well and leave. But that's not the end of it.

Over the next few days the tenants are usually going to be working hard moving in. I try to stop back to see how they're doing and bring them a basket of fruit as a house-warming present. No, it's not necessary. But when you do more than people expect, you get results beyond what you anticipate. This is the extra bit that makes the difference.

A good landlord will continue keeping a business relationship with tenants. This does not mean going overboard and letting the tenant become your best friend. Rather, I mean such things as sending a card at the holidays. I call or stop by every month or two to see how things are going and ask if there's anything I can do to make the place better. Most landlords never come by as long as the tenant doesn't call to complain. That's usually a mistake on two counts. The first is the only time the tenant sees such a landlord is when he or she is complaining and that sours the relationship. Secondly, by stopping by early, you can many times nip problems in the bud and avoid bigger costs down the road.

Help your tenants move in. Make things as easy as possible for them. It will encourage them to do the same for you later on.

CHAPTER 9

The Walk-Through Inspection—Protecting the Deposit

No area of landlord-tenant relations is more contentious with more complaints and lawsuits than that of the return of the deposit. I have yet to find a landlord who doesn't feel that he or she is entitled to at least a portion of the cleaning deposit when the tenant leaves. Similarly, tenants automatically seem to assume that they are entitled to all of the cleaning deposit back.

The truth usually lies somewhere between. I see the reasoning of landlords quite clearly. On the other hand, I've been a tenant once or twice, just enough to know how it feels to not get a cleaning deposit back when I felt I was entitled to it.

I like to tell this story to landlords because when you own and manage property you see so much of the other side of things. These days I'm used to tenants who leave carpets torn and badly stained, walls marked, stoves filthy with grease, toilets and sinks lined with filth . . . well, presumably you're a landlord, too, and I don't have to say more. Frequently, the tenants who leave the biggest mess are the same ones who holler the loudest demanding their cleaning deposit back.

It's easy enough to get permanently inured to tenants' requests for the return of cleaning deposits. However, just keep in mind that there are good tenants out there and even those who don't leave the property up to your standards may indeed have spent considerable time and effort trying to get the place back into shape and, from their perspective, may feel entitled to a sizeable chunk, if not all, of the deposit returned.

TENANT'S STORY

Many years ago when I was right out of college, my wife and I rented a small house. We had a dog, which was okay with the landlord, and put up a $100 cleaning deposit, which in those days was a lot of money for us. We kept the house clean and when we moved, we did a thorough job of cleaning. We shampooed the carpets, waxed the floors, and cleaned everything. Then we asked for our cleaning deposit back.

To this day I remember the landlord walking through the house saying, "Yes, you've done a remarkable job of cleaning up the property. Only, you had a dog in here so there's bound to be hidden damage, particularly to the carpeting. I'm keeping all of the deposit." And that was it. He kept it all. There was really nothing to be done in those days.

I immediately hated landlords (until I became one!) and changed from being cooperative to adversarial. Be careful how you treat your tenants, even those who are moving out. Remember, they'll soon be someone else's tenants, and what goes around, comes around.

WHEN CAN YOU KEEP THE CLEANING DEPOSIT?

The basic rules here have not changed much, although the actual practice has shifted enormously. As landlords know, the rule is the tenants must leave the property in about the same condition as they found it, *normal wear and tear excepted.* It's this last part that often trips up a landlord.

The next story illustrates two points. The first is that you have to be very careful about how you characterize money you withhold from the cleaning deposit. If the tenant can say the damage is caused by normal wear and tear, or in the above case by the landlord's own actions, then they may be entitled to all or a portion of the deposit back. What constitutes damage or normal wear and tear are gray areas.

Second, if you aren't careful the tenants can take you to court, possibly sue you over the cleaning deposit—and win. In the following case, the tenant got only a portion of the cleaning deposit back. However, if you violate state laws regarding the return of a cleaning deposit, you could also be liable for fines.

L A N D L O R D ' S   S T O R Y

Hal rented out a two-bedroom, two-bath apartment to a couple who had children. When the couple moved out, Hal discovered there were marks from colored pencils, crayons and other materials on the bathroom walls. He had hired a cleaning crew to wash down the bathroom walls. However, it turned out that when Hal had painted the apartment a year earlier, he hadn't used high-gloss paint in the bathrooms. Instead, he had use standard flat wall paint. As a consequence, when a cleaning person tried washing the paint, she only smeared the marks. The paint couldn't be washed. So Hal called in a painter who re-painted both bathrooms. Then Hal charged the cost of both the failed cleaning and the re-painting to the tenant by withholding the amount, now up to around $300, from the cleaning deposit.

The tenant protested and eventually took Hal to Small Claims Court. There the tenant agreed that Hal was indeed entitled to the cost of cleaning the bathrooms, about $100. But the tenant claimed Hal was not entitled to the cost of repainting, about $200, because Hal hadn't originally painted the baths with the right kind of paint normally used for bathrooms—the kind that could be washed. The judge agreed and Hal had to return $200 of the deposit to the tenants.

RULES FOR RETURNING A CLEANING DEPOSIT

Most states today require the landlord to do two things regarding a cleaning deposit:

1. If you don't return the entire deposit, you must give the tenant a complete accounting of where the money was spent.
2. You must return the deposit or a portion of it along with the accounting within a maximum period, frequently 14 to 30 days as dictated by the state the property is in.

Just following the guidelines, of course, doesn't mean that you're home free. If the tenants disagree with your accounting, particularly the amount you have withheld, they can take you to court, usually Small Claims Court, and sue to recover all or part of their cleaning deposit. Because many courts these days tend to look with favor on tenants' complaints in these matters, it's now up to you to substantiate your claims for damage.

> **Hint:** If the tenant leaves the place in a mess and you hire someone to clean it up, generally speaking you can deduct the cost of the cleanup from the cleaning deposit. On the other hand, if you clean up the place yourself, while you can deduct your cost of materials, you probably cannot deduct a figure for your time spent. Thus, it often pays to hire someone else to do the work.

DOCUMENTING THE CONDITION OF THE PROPERTY

Probably the best thing you can do to avoid arguments and lawsuits when the tenant moves out is to document *before* and *after.* You need to show how the property looked *before* the tenant moved in and then how it looked *after* the tenant moved out.

While it is true that arguments can grow over the cost of certain repairs, the most common area of disagreement is over what the property looked like before. Usually the landlord says the unit was in perfect shape while the tenant claims it was a mess to begin with. Who's right? Keep in mind that today many courts tend to favor tenants' claims over those of landlords.

Film and Video Documentation

Some landlords have taken to recording the initial condition of the property through the use of a camera and/or a camcorder. The idea is that before renting you walk through the property, visually preparing a record of the condition of floors, walls, appliances, and so on. Thus, when the tenant moves out and claims that the property was not clean or newly painted or whatever, you have a visual record to prove otherwise.

There are, however, certain problems inherent in a visual record which courts as well as insurance companies have come to recognize, namely, image manipulation through such computer programs as Adobe Photo-Shop. Further, even if the image itself is not computer-manipulated, adjusting the elements of lighting and camera angle can make a scratched wall look perfect. While no ethical landlord would do such a thing, nevertheless, simply because it's possible has cast visual records into doubt. In short, taking "before" and "after" pictures may be considered unreliable.

Further, since you don't know where damage might occur, you would have to photograph everything in detail in order to be sure that you have a clean "before" picture—a daunting task.

> **Hint:** Taking pictures of actual damage after the fact is worthwhile. Pictures can demonstrate that the property has, indeed, been damaged, helping your case immensely when the tenant says there's been no damage. Just don't count on the pictures to say who caused the damage.

If you choose to go ahead with videos of the property, keep in mind that there's the inconvenience of playback. You need a playback VCR (the camcorder itself will do), and a TV set. Setting this up in a Small Claims courtroom can be a hassle. (However, I do know landlords who shoot VHS video and then bring a small VCR/TV combo right with them to court to show a small claims judge just what damage exists.) Of course, you have to "index" the tape so you can move just to the images you want to show. Most judges aren't pleased to wait while you search through an hour of video for just the right scene.

Disputed Videos

Of course, with any kind of visual records the tenant can dispute *when* you shot the original saying the property wasn't in that condition when they moved in. They can claim your "before" video was shot years ago when the rental was new. When they moved in, it was already damaged and dirty.

One landlord I know attempts to solve this problem by having an independent person, such as a neighbor, walk through the video saying the date and time.

In short, visual records can be helpful, but in my experience their aid is more in the area of secondary support to back up what you've otherwise demonstrated to be the case, particularly with damage after the move out.

If a visual record isn't enough, how do you demonstrate the condition of the rental before the tenants move in?

What's worked for me and a lot of property managers over the years is a proper "walk-through inspection sheet." The walk-through inspection sheet goes a long way toward substantiating the true condition of the rental. Check out the inspection sheet in the appendix.

WHAT ARE WALK-THROUGH INSPECTION SHEETS?

Walk-through inspection sheets are written documentation *signed by both the landlord and the tenants.* It's very hard for a tenant to later say that a wall was marked or a stove was filthy when they have signed that both were clean and in good condition when they moved in.

The idea is that after you've approved the tenants and received the rent, but before handing over the keys and as a condition of renting, they must go with you through the property checking off the sheets.

The tenants are made aware that the purpose of the walk-through inspection sheet is to document the condition of the property before taking possession and it's to their advantage to note any problems. You'll almost never find a tenant unwilling to go through this process.

Go Room by Room

There is a walk-through sheet for each room—each bedroom, bathroom, dining room, living room, hallway, kitchen, and other area. There should be no area of the house left out, including closets.

The sheets note the condition of the walls, ceilings, floors, windows, screens, fixtures, and appliances—in short, everything in the house.

The sheets specifically state that each item is *without damage, and clean, having no marks except as noted.* There is a place where any dirt, marks, scratches, or damage can and should be noted. Tenants should not only sign at the end of the list, but initial each sheet and initial important items such as the stove (a big area of contention over cleanliness), the sink, the refrigerator, and so on.

CONDUCTING THE WALK-THROUGH

There's a whole psychology involved in the walk-through. Remember, it's done before the tenants move anything into the property; before the tenants take possession. As a result, there isn't any pressure (as there is at move-out time) for the tenants to worry you're going to say they did anything. Rather, they are looking for faults and you, as the landlord, are often having to defend the condition of the property! It's another reason to be sure that each time you rent a property, it's in tip-top shape.

Further, there's usually an upbeat feeling of good cheer during the walk-through. After all, the tenants have nothing to worry about—they haven't moved in yet and can't be blamed for anything wrong. Further, since the tenancy is just starting, they naturally want to be on a good footing with you. So, at this time, they are least likely to exaggerate a problem. After all, if they insist there's a big hole in the carpet and there's no hole there, you aren't going to be too likely to give them the key to move in.

On the other hand, most tenants will be scrupulously careful going over these sheets with you. They will carefully point out every mark, scratch, tear, and other dirty or damaged part of the rental unit. After all, they full well understand that anything that goes on this sheet won't come back to haunt them when they move out.

Getting an Accurate Description

It is absolutely necessary that you use precise language to describe any exceptions to "clean and undamaged" that you write down. For example, there may be a mark in a wall caused by the previous tenant having hit it with a dresser while moving out. If you write down, "back wall of bedroom is marked," you could be in for real trouble. When this tenant moves out, that wall could be covered from floor to ceiling with marks and when you protest, the tenant will point to the walk-through saying, "See, you wrote down that the wall was marked!"

Be specific. Write, "small single mark on back wall approximately two inches long by half an inch wide." That pretty much limits the claim that the whole wall was marked.

Don't Forget Safety Features

Almost every area of the country today requires that a rental be equipped with smoke detectors. The move-in walk-through is an excellent place to note not only that your rental unit has one, but that it is in working condition. Have tenants sign (or initial) that they've seen the smoke detector and tested it themselves.

Some locations also require fire extinguishers. Be sure the tenant signs that they have noted the location of the extinguisher and that it is full and in working condition.

Working with the Tenant

There are, of course, bound to be areas of dispute. One of the most common is the carpeting. The tenant will say that the carpeting looks old and worn. You may say that it's nearly new and fresh. How do you come up with a description that you both can live with?

One answer that my property manager friend has is to list (1) the age of the carpet, as evidenced by her bill-of-sale, and (2) the last time it was cleaned, as evidenced by her invoice from the carpet cleaning company. It's hard for a tenant to argue with these two items. Then, any specific damage or wear, such as cigarette burns or stains, can be noted as to size and location.

Try using the walk-through inspection sheet. It takes a a little extra time, but it can be well worth it later on.

Keeping the Good Tenant Happy

Ask any landlord to describe a good tenant and you'll be told, "They pay their rent promptly!" True enough. But what if that "good" tenant moves out after six months or complains all the time? The other elements that landlords often forget to mention is that the good tenant stays in the rental for year after year and doesn't complain a lot. Longevity and tolerance is likewise important.

A good tenant—one who pays on time, doesn't complain, and stays there a long while—is like the goose who lays the golden eggs. You want to keep them happy. How do you do that?

KEEP A MAINTENANCE AND REPLACEMENT SCHEDULE

One of the biggest criticisms of landlords that good tenants have is that while they pay their rents regularly, the landlord doesn't maintain and upkeep their rental on a regular basis. After all, carpets wear out (particularly the inexpensive kind found in many rentals). Kitchen and bath floors get scratched and worn. Appliances not only break, but simply become obsolete or worn out. "Why," the good tenant reasonably asks, "will the landlord put new carpeting in for a brand new tenant, when he won't do it for me, when I've been living here and paying rent regularly for years?"

As a landlord, it's your responsibility to maintain and replace items that wear out, especially for the good tenant. Just because a tenant doesn't complain doesn't mean he or she isn't concerned, or won't take action and move.

LANDLORD'S STORY

Jimmy had an older apartment building with 24 units. He maintained a regular schedule of replacing carpeting and linoleum and repainting. Every five years he would go through a unit and replace both and repaint as needed. Of course, the new carpeting and flooring was not expensive, but it looked good. And the painting made the units look terrific. Jimmy did this regardless if the tenants were new or existing.

As a result, he had one of the lowest turnover rates in the area. Indeed, some of the tenants had been in the building since it was new, nearly 20 years earlier!

Yes, he had the regular expense of maintenance. But, he saved the much more costly expense of repeated tenant turnover.

Many landlords feel that the only time they'll replace such items as carpeting and paint is when there's a tenant turnover. As a result, existing tenants get dissatisfied, move out, and there's a lot of turnover. Indeed, by not taking care of the good tenants, you can increase both your turnover and your maintenance and replacement costs.

MAINTAINING A POSITIVE ENVIRONMENT

One reason good tenants will want to stay a long time is that they like the environment. This usually means three things:

1. The common areas, such as walks, gardens, and parking spaces, are attractive. This usually means employing a good gardener as well as black-topping asphalt or repairing concrete on a regular basis.
2. There are no loud parties or noisy tenants. In some areas, this is unavoidable. But in others, it's something that the landlords work

hard to achieve. I know of one apartment complex with 360 units where strict noise restrictions are applied. In spite of the density, the landlord won't tolerate loud music or noisy parties, certainly not after 10 PM. As a result, this complex has a far lower vacancy rate than competing units.

3. The property is maintained in a neat and clean manner. The landlord or a manager is around to sweep leaves, pick up and clean up debris, and to see that everything is always in order.

Keep the environment appealing and the tenants will want to stay.

DEAL WITH PROBLEMS PROMPTLY

Then there's the matter of legitimate complaint calls. A good tenant calls up and says that the faucet in the bathroom is dripping and it's keeping him awake at night. What do you do? Simple. You or your help goes there the next day to fix it. You've got a good tenant. You don't want to lose her because of a leaking faucet.

Or a tenant calls up and says the garbage disposal is broken, only it's Saturday and you can't get anyone out until Monday. What do you do? You sympathize, say you're sorry, and explain that you can't have someone come out until after the weekend. Most tenants will be understanding.

If it's a good tenant who rarely complains, but says that she's having dinner guests that night and she can't use her sink, what do you do? Get it fixed right away. Do it yourself or pay extra to have someone do it. No, I'm not recommending this on a regular basis. But tenants have crises, too. And if it's not their fault and it occurs very rarely, take care of it. They'll remember what you did (or didn't do) for them.

Hint: Many old-time landlords may take issue with the above. Their philosophy is that the only things tenants remember are what you do wrong, so why go out of your way for them? Having been in the business many years, I think that's too jaded a perspective. I've had far, far more good tenants than bad and I firmly believe that a large part of that has to do with treating them as I would want to be treated.

BE FRIENDLY WITH YOUR TENANTS, BUT NOT TOO FRIENDLY

It's possible to get too friendly with tenants. While it is important to get to know your tenants so that if something goes awry, you'll know with whom you're dealing, you don't want to become their friends. A friendly tenant can turn into a pest.

Just as the tenants want to have the "quiet enjoyment" of your property, you as a landlord normally want to be isolated from the tenants' lives and small problems. Except in unusual circumstances (such as when you rent to relatives—something I do not recommend), you want to be

LANDLORD'S STORY

Sally is a landlady who owns several houses. Not long ago Sally had a problem tenant. This tenant wasn't paying late or messing up the property—the tenant paid promptly and was extremely neat and clean.

Rather, this tenant was overly friendly. Sally had at first made a point of getting to know the tenant to the point where they exchanged recipes and occasionally chatted on the phone.

However, the tenant began calling Sally at all hours with concerns that were trivial. For example, the tenant called Sally at 10:30 one night to say a faucet in the kitchen was dripping. That's certainly something that needs to get fixed. But it's not an emergency requiring fixing at night. Sally sent someone over the next day to take care of it.

Another night at 11:30 the tenant called Sally to say that a doorstop had come off and the door handle was in danger of making a hole in the wall (a fairly common problem with rental property). Sally had someone go out a few days later. In the meantime, the tenant called twice more about the "problem."

In fact, there was hardly a week that went by that the tenant didn't call once or twice with minor problems from a broken screen to a sprinkler head that was aimed the wrong direction.

Needless to say, Sally was ready to kick the tenant out because of the intrusions into her life. But the tenant always paid on time, often in advance of the time the rent was due. And the tenant was always so friendly when she called, treating Sally like an old acquaintance asking for a small favor.

Eventually the only way Sally could solve the problem was, at an additional cost, to have a management firm take over the property. Then she changed her phone number!

friendly, but not be friends, with your tenants. You want to be able to drop by or call up on the phone and hear a hearty, "How're you doing!" on their end. But you don't want to see them every other day. You want your tenants to respect you, not love you.

GETTING OFF ON THE RIGHT FOOT

In the above example, Sally initially struck up the wrong relationship with the tenant. The tenant was a single woman who was apparently lonely and looking for friends. Sally, being gregarious, naturally took the tenant under her wing and by the time the woman moved in, she considered Sally a kindred spirit. Sally, on the other hand, simply thought she was being friendly.

At first, Sally responded to the frequent calls with her normal friendly demeanor, never realizing this was being misinterpreted by the tenant. Soon the one-way relationship was established that was driving Sally crazy. So she had to pay to get someone else to take over management of the property.

Hint: Always be friendly with your tenants; never be their friends.

A BUSINESS PROPOSITION

From the first, you must establish that although you may be a friendly person, the landlord/tenant relationship is basically one of business. Yes, as a landlord you are available for handling problems that occur with the property—at normal business hours of 9 to 5, or in the early evening if you work during the day. If the tenant calls late in the evening, it has to be a real emergency threatening the habitability of the property.

One landlord I know has cards printed up with his name and address on them as well as his business hours. Because he works during the day, his business hours are from 6:00 PM to 9:00 PM. This phone line is just for rental calls and he has an answering machine on it to take calls at other times. He frequently checks in on the answering machine during the day and can monitor calls after 9:00 PM, so he is able to keep up-to-date on any tenant requests or emergencies without having them intrude on his regular work or his personal life.

THE UNREASONABLE TENANT

Sometimes, it's more than just keeping a good tenant happy. Sometimes, it's dealing with a tenant who pays on time, but is simply unreasonable.

An unreasonable tenant may call at all hours of the day or night with problems that may or may not be legitimate complaints. For example, tenants may call complaining about the color of paint in the living room—it doesn't go with their furniture and they want you to repaint. Or the sliding screen door leading to the patio doesn't slide easily enough on its track. Yes, it works fine and doesn't come off the track, but it doesn't function as smoothly as the tenant would like. Or a closet door creaks when it is opened. Or the dishwasher isn't getting the dishes clean enough.

The list can go on and on, but you get the idea. The demands are in the gray area. They certainly aren't threatening the habitability of the property. They don't qualify as true repairs. They aren't exactly alterations. They are sort of, but not quite, improvements. In short, they are unreasonable.

DRAWING A LINE

If you allow these "good" tenants to have their way, you will spend the entire period of the tenancy (and probably a great deal of money) making unnecessary changes to the property.

What you need to do is to let tenants know what your boundaries are, what you are willing to do, and what you're not willing to do. You need to draw a line and state you won't step over it.

When I get the first such request from tenants who are paying rent on time, assuming it isn't too costly, I usually go along and have the change or the work done. However, while it is being done, I tell the tenants that this is not something I feel obligated to do, but I'm just doing it because they're such good tenants. In the future, however, I won't do any more such work.

I might say something such as, "I'm lubricating all of the door hinges so they won't squeak. I'm doing this because you're such good tenants.

However, in any house, door hinges will tend to squeak. In the future you'll have to take care of this yourself. Of course, I'll always fix anything that actually breaks, such as a broken furnace or a leaking faucet. But squeaky door hinges or a sliding screen door that works okay, but doesn't move quite as smoothly as you want, or something along those lines, I don't consider broken items and I won't fix them. If you want them changed, I can arrange to have the work done, but you'll have to pay for it yourself."

I've given the tenant my boundaries. While some tenants might continue to "push the envelope" to see what more they can wring out of me, most quickly understand the situation and stop being demanding.

For those persistent complainers, doing one small job and sending them a bill for it, even if it's only $10 or so, quickly ends the demands.

It pays to let others know where you stand. Once in a great while this policy might cost you a "good" tenant, but the rest of the time you'll sleep peacefully at night without pesty phone calls. Keeping a good tenant happy doesn't mean acceding to their every demand.

CHAPTER 11

When the Tenant Damages or Doesn't Maintain Your Property

There are two components to getting the tenant to take good care of your property. The first is clarity—you have to make absolutely sure that the tenants are clear about what they are supposed to do. The second is to have reasonable expectations; tenants must reasonably be able to accomplish what you and they agree upon.

THE TENANT WHO DOESN'T KEEP UP THE PROPERTY

In the case of renting out single-family homes, it's often the case that the landlord expects the tenant to keep the premises clean, mow the lawn, trim the trees, water the grounds, even keep up the pool. In general the tenant is expected to maintain the property the way you feel it should be maintained.

Your first job, however, should be to determine whether it's an unreasonable expectation on your part or an impossible task for the tenant. Checking out those two questions will often do far more than ranting and raving at the tenant for not doing the work.

At the time you sign the rental agreement with the tenant, it's not enough that you both agree on who is to take care of what maintenance. It's also important that the agreement be reasonable and that the tenant be able to handle what you've both agreed upon.

L A N D L O R D ' S   S T O R Y

Hal wrote into his leases that his tenants were to pay for all utilities, including water. In addition, on one enormous property in particular, he also emphasized that the tenants were to maintain the lawn and shrubs in the front and rear yards in good condition.

Hal rented the property during the early summer and a couple of months after the tenants moved in he drove by, only to see that the lawn was brown and thinning and the leaves were falling off the shrubs. He stopped his car, jumped out and ran up to the door, startling the tenants by demanding to know why they were killing his lawn and shrubs.

They shrugged and said they had watered heavily the first month, until they got a $145 water bill. Since then, they were only watering minimally. If Hal wanted to pay the water bill, they'd water all he wanted. Otherwise, they couldn't afford more.

Hal ranted and raved and threatened to throw them out for violating their lease. A month-and-a-half later they moved on their own, leaving a dead lawn and dying shrubs that made rerenting much more difficult.

Never ask tenants to take on more maintenance than they can handle. The above rule is obvious in the case of watering lawns. Many landlords will automatically pay for water just to be sure that lawns and shrubs are adequately maintained. Most landlords feel it's cheaper in the long run to pay the water bills than it is to run the risk of having the tenants let the greenery die out.

One exception is in drought areas where there might be a hefty penalty for using too much water. There, you might want to give the tenants a "water allowance." You might pay $30 of the water bill or whatever a month for each month that you come by and see that the yard is green.

THE MESSY TENANT

I've had tenants who kept the inside of the house or apartment so clean that the old expression, "you could eat off the floor" was almost no exaggeration. And, I've had tenants who made such a mess out of the premises that you had trouble walking between rooms, having to step over piles of debris.

Naturally, I, like you, would prefer the former tenant. But if you are in this business long enough, you'll get the latter. What do you do about the messy tenant? Some people are just not very neat and there's nothing you can do about that. For example, they may allow clothes to fall everywhere. (I once had a tenant who had a "clothes room." That meant that all her clothes were dumped on the floor of one room, some clean, some dirty, some needing ironing—you get the idea. I swear that at times the clothes in that room were three feet or more deep!)

That's not the way our family is run. But it's also none of my business how other families are run and I know that. As long as there was no damage to the property (and there wasn't), I couldn't say anything, except weakly point out a possible fire hazard. This is another good reason for stopping by your rental periodically and walking through. It doesn't have to be a formal appointment although technically you do need to make an appointment to get in. Just drop by and ask how things are. Mention that there was an old leak in one of the sinks and you want to check to be sure it's fixed. Or you want to change the furnace filter. If you're on good relations with the tenant, you'll most certainly be asked in.

It's important that you don't insist your tenants follow your lifestyle or your family rules. You will only be ineffectual and frustrated.

MESS VERSUS DAMAGE

Damage is quite different from mess. When the property has been damaged, you must make it clear to the tenant that they must correct the problem themselves, or you will correct it and charge them for it. In other words, the property must be returned to its original state.

Hint: Your rental agreement should always contain a clause allowing you to enter and examine the property upon giving the tenant adequate notice, usually 24 hours.

The difference between damage that must be corrected immediately and that which may be corrected over time has to do with safety and liability. And damage which poses a safety hazard must be corrected immediately.

Typical damage requiring immediate correction includes:

- Broken glass
- Broken sinks, stoves, faucets, heaters, floor tiles

L A N D L O R D ' S   S T O R Y

Sally's tenants called one day to say that their son had driven a baseball through one of two large plate glass windows in the back of the residence. They wanted it fixed immediately, as jagged pieces of glass were all over.

Sally immediately sent over a glazer who took care of the window for $350. Then she paid for it out of the tenant's security deposit and sent a bill for that amount requesting the tenants bring their security deposit back up to its full level. They were outraged at the price (it was safety glass), but agreed to pay.

The real story started a month later when Sally dropped by for a surprise visit. The tenants invited her in and she immediately noticed that the other plate glass window was also broken. (Apparently their son was a strong, but not highly talented baseball player.) However, they had not reported it. Instead, they had taken several sheets of transparent tape and taped up the broken shards, thus holding the broken window together. They casually mentioned that it was a lot cheaper than replacing it.

Sally said it was a tremendous safety hazard and told them it had to be fixed. She also immediately sent them a note repeating what she had said. She gave them one week to correct the problem on their own, or she would hire someone to come in and fix the window and charge it to them.

They took care of the window. But, they no longer invited her inside when she casually dropped by. So now she makes an appointment to stop by once every other month or so. In any event, there are no more broken windows.

- Large holes in walls
- Broken walkways

Typical damage requiring correction, but not immediately includes:

- Paint or heavy crayon marks on walls, often caused by allowing children to run free with crayons or paints. (Crayons in particular can be hard to remove because they often stain right through wall paint. If you don't catch this quickly, it may occur on many more walls during the tenancy.)
- Small amounts of animal urine or feces anywhere inside the property except in a special animal litter box.

- Torn carpets, drapes, broken cabinet doors, etc.
- Normal wear and tear including small holes to walls (particularly behind door knobs), dirty drapes, window coverings, sinks, stoves, etc.

MAINTENANCE TASKS YOU SHOULD LET THE TENANT DO

There are several maintenance tasks that tenants usually expect to do and that landlords assign to them.

Yard Maintenance

When you are renting out a single family house, a duplex (two units), or a triplex (three units), it is quite common to have the tenants take care of the yard, at least the sides and back. If a tenant balks at this, a good way of handling it is to offer to hire a gardener, but to add the cost to the monthly rent. Some landlords ask a higher rent and then offer to negotiate a lower one if the tenant will agree to take care of the yard work. A better solution is to send the tenant a separate check each month than to simply settle on a lower rent payment. Then if the tenant stops taking care of the lawn in an acceptable fashion, you don't need to renegotiate again—just terminate the lawn care agreement.

When you are renting smaller multiple units—small apartment buildings or, in some cases duplexes, triplexes, or even fourplexes where there are common areas—you may want to give one tenant an allowance for sweeping, cleaning, and, if the total areas are small, mowing and gardening. This avoids problems of who is supposed to take care of what area. For bigger buildings, it is almost always advisable to hire a gardener.

Minimal Plumbing Work

This is also sometimes taken care of by tenants who express a willingness to do this and who have the ability. This includes unstopping plugged toilets or drains, changing washers in faucets, cleaning heating filters, and so on. I have one tenant who is more than happy to do all of these things just so I won't bother to come around. This tenant loves his privacy.

MAINTENANCE TASKS YOU SHOULD NEVER LET THE TENANT DO

The list here is far longer than the "allow to do" list.

Cleaning Out Plugged Drain Lines

If plugged sinks and pipes don't respond to a plumber's helper, they probably need a long mechanical rooter device. This is best handled by professionals.

Painting

What do you do when the tenants call up and say that they've been living in the property for three years now and the bedrooms, living room, and dining room need to be repainted? The paint wasn't in wonderful condition (as you agree) when they moved in and it's time to repaint.

However, they know that repainting is costly, so they have a plan. If you will pay for the paint, they will do the work. Of course, you'll have control over the colors they choose.

The response to this seemingly fair request varies according to landlords and their experiences. Many landlords will acquiesce. I personally do not.

The problem that I have found is that most people are lousy painters. (I include one of my sons and most of my relatives in this category.) The average person does not do a good job of covering the surface evenly with paint. They leave streaks, drips, and bare spots. They get spray, drips, and puddles on the floor and carpeting. In short, to have the average person paint my property usually means that not only will I have to have it repainted to get a good job, but I may also need to repair damage (such as paint on the carpet). Further, once I agree to them doing it, any repainting and repairs are probably going to be out of my pocket. Once you give your permission to paint, you'll get a big argument from the tenant when you later try to charge them for cleanup.

If a property needs repainting, either I paint it myself or I hire a professional. It usually doesn't take me long or cost me much, and I'm assured of the result.

If, however, you feel that you want to try saving money by allowing the tenant to paint, here's a suggestion: buy the paint, rollers, and brushes yourself. Always buy the best quality. The best goes on easier, covers better, and improves your odds of getting a good job.

Washing Walls

Walls get dirty over time. Washing them only makes the dirt stand out more. The reason is that you can't really wash a wall very effectively. You can only wash a portion of it, usually the lower half and then only sections. That means that where the washed and unwashed areas meet, there will be visible dirt lines. I always discourage tenants from washing walls. When they are dirty, they need to be repainted.

Major Repair Jobs

Major repairs include the water heater, furnace, air conditioner, compactor, garbage disposal, etc. Your liability if the tenant gets hurt doing work you authorize could be enormous. Also, a tenant who has good intentions may not be competent to do a good job.

Taking Care of Pools and Spas

Often the tenants are willing, but the expertise and follow-up is weak. Pools and spas require at least weekly cleaning and chemical correction. Let them go even an extra week or two (particularly during the hot summer months) and damaging algae can quickly grow. Besides, necessary regular cleaning of filters can be hard, dirty work, something which most tenants won't want to do. Either you or a pool service should take care of this.

THE TENANT WHO WANTS TO IMPROVE THE PROPERTY

Occasionally tenants will come to you with a request that sounds very reasonable. One of the most common I've run into has to do with lawn sprinklers in single family homes.

L A N D L O R D ' S   S T O R Y

Our poor friend Hal had a most unfortunate experience here. He owned a property with a large pool. He was paying $75 a month to a pool service company to maintain it. One day his tenant suggested that Hal turn over the pool maintenance to the tenant. "It only costs $5 or $10 worth of chemicals each month and I'm here anyway. Just cut the rent by $40 a month. We'll both save money that way."

Hal jumped at the opportunity.

When Hal next came back to the property several months later, he was aghast at the pool's condition. It had been bright blue. Now it was green, with yellow and black algae growing profusely on the sides. He demanded to know what had happened.

The tenant sheepishly confessed he had tried to save money on chlorine and probably hadn't added enough. But, he told Hal, he'd cure it.

Hal came back a month later and it was even worse. The tenant admitted he couldn't handle the pool and said Hal had better take back its maintenance.

The real problem is that when Hal called back his pool service company, they told him they would have to drain the pool, acid wash it several times and even replace some of the filtration equipment. It was going to cost him close to $1,000.

The tenants are usually responsible for watering the lawn (unless you have a gardener). However, it's a time-consuming burden to run a hose out and turn on a portable sprinkler head. The tenants say that what's needed is underground sprinklers. If you will pay for the materials, and perhaps a minimum hourly wage, they will do the work.

Automatic sprinklers, with an electric timer to turn them on automatically, are the only way to assurance that your lawn will be watered regularly. You need sprinklers and this may seem like a request from heaven.

My advice is not to give into the temptation of having the tenants do the work. Although installing a sprinkler system only requires rudimentary plumbing skills, it does require some skill—and a great deal of hard work. In most locales it also requires a building department permit. (You will, after all, be tapping into the potable water supply.)

And if the tenants give up on the project, finishing a botched job is tougher than doing it correct right from the start. Yes, it does cost money to do it right. But do you really want it done wrong?

The same problems come up with other projects that your tenants may come up with such as building a deck, a patio cover, adding a greenhouse window, converting a bedroom to a family room (or vice-versa) or anything else. My advice is to just say *no*.

BEWARE OF DEDUCTING PAYMENTS FOR WORK FROM RENT

As noted earlier, never give rent deductions. For example, don't reduce the rent by $30 if the tenant waters the yard properly. Almost immediately the tenant will think of the rental rate as $30 less and will forget about what has to be done to earn that money. On the other hand, if each month you send a check for $30 to the tenant, made payable to the water company (for watering the lawn and shrubs), you have a continuing incentive that is tied directly to the maintenance task you want accomplished.

Also, if you reduce rent, forgo the acceptance of rent, or pay a tenant directly for performing work such as maintaining a pool, you could actually be setting up an employee/employer relationship as defined by federal and perhaps even state law. If such a relationship exists, you could be responsible for withholding tax, workers' compensation and other employer responsibilities.

WHEN THE TENANT MAKES CHANGES WITHOUT PERMISSION

Probably one of the most shocking rental experiences I ever had was many years ago when I stopped by a rental to collect the rent one day and was asked in by a friendly tenant, who proudly displayed her new color scheme. I gasped in surprise and horror to see the walls and ceilings all painted a very shiny—and probably very permanent—deep purple.

The tenant saw my distress and immediately pointed out how well her black leather couch went with the new color scheme, as did her very dark green throw rug. I had to agree that, indeed, the colors did seem in harmony.

What I was seeing, however, and the tenant wasn't, was my inability to rerent when she moved out. Normally light colors make the place seem airy and roomy and are attractive to most people. There aren't many prospective tenants who are willing to move into a dark, cavelike dwelling. And painting over a dark color with a light color can be next to impossible, short of putting on three or four coats—an expensive proposition.

I dutifully informed the proud tenant that the rental agreement specifically forbade painting without the approval of the landlord and in any event, the landlord had to agree to the colors. The tenant just scoffed at that and said something to the effect of, "Who wouldn't like their place repainted and by the way, what's wrong with the color?"

What was I to do? After all, it was already painted!

I duly noted that when the tenant moved out, the unit would have to be repainted back to the original color and that the cost of that would come out of the security/cleaning deposit, if there was enough. Then I left, hoping this tenant would stay there a very, very long time.

AVOIDING UNAPPROVED REPAIRS OR IMPROVEMENTS

In the above example, the tenant disregarded a written part of the rental agreement and altered the property without the landlord's consent. Unfortunately, as noted, I didn't find out until the deed was done and by then, it was too late to do anything except corrective work.

The idea is to nip this sort of thing in the bud. You want to head off unapproved work before it starts. You do this by emphasizing your expectations from the very beginning, when the tenant first moves in.

Today when a tenant moves in, amongst other things discussed, I emphasize that there are to be no alterations, improvements, or repairs to the property without the specific written approval of the landlord. I even highlight this part of the rental agreement and have the tenant initial it, indicating that they have indeed seen it.

CHAPTER 12

Making Repairs

It goes without saying that as a landlord, you're going to have to make some repairs to the property. A dishwasher goes out, a window screen tears, a fence comes down. You need to fix it.

Sometimes it's covered by insurance (as is often the case, for example, when the wind blows down a fence). But most times it isn't and you have to pay for the repairs. That's when it gets expensive.

Build cushion into your rental investment so you can afford to make repairs when needed. If you haven't, then you'll have to come up with the money out of your pocket.

The one thing a landlord cannot afford to do, however, is to let things go so far that, eventually, the tenant is forced to make the repairs. If this happens, you no longer have control over the amount the repair will cost, how it will be done, what damage doing the repair might cause, and where the money to pay for it will come from.

TENANTS' REPAIR RIGHTS

Those new to being a landlord may wonder about tenants making repairs. After all, they're living there; why shouldn't they repair the premises? It's the difference between owning and renting. You profit from the repairs; presumably the tenant does not. For this reason many states have enacted laws that allow the tenant to make necessary repairs, if you fail to do so, and then deduct the cost of those repairs from the next rent payment.

The reason for such laws is that in the past unscrupulous landlords have rented out premises where there were inadequate water or sanitary facilities or heating or some other item necessary to make the premises habitable. The tenants paid the rent, then didn't receive the water or heat or working toilet that they were entitled to. In order to get things working, in the past, they might have to make the repairs themselves, out of their own pocket, thus improving the landlord's property. To secure payment from the landlord, they would then have to go to court where the outcome was always in doubt.

The tenant protection laws of many states, on the other hand, provide that if the landlord does not make repairs that are necessary to bring the property up to a condition fit for human occupancy in a timely fashion, the tenants can take self help measures. They can make the repairs themselves and then deduct the cost from the next month's rent.

Usually there are conditions tied to this self-help remedy.

- The tenant must have informed the landlord of the problem.
- The landlord must refuse to correct it in a reasonable amount of time.
- The repairs usually must not cost more than one month's rent.
- The tenant cannot use this self-help method more than once or twice a year. (Check with your state department of real estate to see the exact rules in your state.)

WHY NOT LET THE TENANT DO IT AND DEDUCT FROM THE RENT?

At first glance, you might wonder what's the problem with having the tenant do the repair. After all, isn't the landlord getting necessary work done, without having to take the trouble to do it himself or herself?

What the following story illustrates is the reason you don't want to have your tenants make repairs. Their objectives are inevitably going to be different from yours. They want it done as quickly as possible and cost is no object. You want it done soon, of course, but as inexpensively as possible.

Here's another story about my pal, Hal, the worst landlord I ever knew. Hal had a number of properties including a small house that he owned and rented out. One evening fairly late the tenants called to say that the water heater had developed a leak. Water was running out the bottom of it and into the garage. They had called the gas company who told them the heater was no longer operative; they had shut it down. Now, the tenants had no hot water.

Hal, who was home enjoying a ball game with a glass of wine, one of his favorite pleasures, told them, "Yeah, yeah, I'll get back to you on it." He continued to watch the game and promptly forgot about the tenants.

They called again the next morning, that afternoon, and the following evening. Hal decided they were being pests, particularly since he felt they weren't paying enough rent anyhow. So he ignored them.

A few days passed. The tenants stopped calling and Hal, involved in other pursuits, promptly forgot about the whole thing . . . until the beginning of the next month when the tenants sent in the rent, or should have. The rent was $650 a month and they sent him a check for $23 and a paid bill for $627 for having a new water heater installed. Needless to say, Hal went through the roof.

He raced over to the property and demanded to know what was going on. He had no intention of paying $627 for a water heater. He hadn't authorized it. Even if he did, he was sure he could get one installed for a couple of hundred dollars. Why, he could install it himself for half that!

The tenants, who had checked with a local real estate agent, calmly explained that they had called him seven times over a three-day period and he had not responded. They could not live in the property without hot water. So, under the "repairs by tenants" laws of their state, they had fixed the problem. Because they felt it was an emergency, they called a service person who came right out and did the work. They told Hal he would be pleased to know that the new water heater was one of the best produced and, of course, one of the most expensive.

BEWARE OF TENANTS WHO JUMP THE GUN

While most tenants may not be aware of their rights here, many are. And a few may want to take advantage of the landlord. They may go ahead and do all sorts of things to the property, such as paint, add new flooring or sinks or whatever, and then deduct it from the rent. Your only recourse may be to go to court to get your money back from them.

Avoid this problem by making clear both your and the tenant's responsibilities with regard to repairs. You don't want any gray area. To that end, a clause such as the one following is often inserted into the rental agreement, and then read aloud or otherwise pointed out to the tenant at the time they move in.

Repairs and Improvements

Tenants agree not to alter, redecorate, or make repairs to the dwelling, except as provided by law, without first obtaining the owner's (landlord's) specific written permission.

Owner (landlord) agrees to undertake as soon as possible any and all repairs necessary to make the premises habitable and to correct any defects that are hazardous to the health and safety of the occupants, *upon notification by tenants of the problem.* If the owner (landlord) cannot reasonably complete such repairs within three days, he (she) shall keep tenants informed of the work progress.

This sort of language puts the tenants on notice that they are not to make repairs by themselves and that they must contact the landlord if any problems occur requiring repair. As soon as the landlord learns of a problem, necessary repairs will be made.

Why let the tenant know you're going to promptly take care of the work? After all, you may be short of funds when the work is required and may want to let it slip a week or so. The reason is simple: if you don't do it and the premises become uninhabitable, as noted earlier, the tenants may have the legal right to make repairs themselves and then deduct the cost from the rent. As we've seen, you don't want that to happen.

Of course, sometimes repairs can't be completed immediately. Parts must be ordered or work cannot be started immediately. When that happens you must keep the tenants informed as to what's going on, so they don't make the assumption that nothing's happening and attempt the repairs themselves.

WHAT IF THE PROPERTY BECOMES UNINHABITABLE?

One of the implicit requirements of renting is that you provide a property that is habitable. If there's no water, sewerage, heat, or light, if there are broken windows, a leaking roof, or any other problem that can be considered to render the premises unfit for human habitation, you can't collect the rent. That's why you've got to fix all serious problems quickly.

L A N D L O R D ' S   S T O R Y

A landlord friend had a single-family home rented to a couple who couldn't change a light bulb. They called him for everything.

One night they called to say there was a mouse in the house. He said he'd be out the next day with a trap.

Before he could get there, he got a panicked call from the tenants saying a big rat was in their bedroom and it had them cornered on one side of the bed. They couldn't get out. What should they do?

The landlord drove over only to discover that the rat had disappeared, and so had the tenants. They took a room at a motel saying the premises was uninhabitable because of vermin.

The landlord put down a couple of traps and then hired an exterminator. Three days later the exterminator explained that some tree rats had gotten into the roof and built a nest. A few baby rats had gotten into the house. No big deal and he was taking care of the problem. But it would be another week or so before he could be sure all of the rats were gone.

The landlord informed the tenants who said they'd be back a week later. They were and presented the landlord with a bill for the motel costs!

Ultimately, the landlord did not have to pay the motel costs for the tenants, but he lost nearly two weeks' rent plus the cost of extermination. Who's to say how much it would have cost him if he hadn't acted promptly?

When the Rent Is Late

Sooner or later, every landlord experiences late rent payments. Perhaps you're currently having this problem and are looking for a solution. If so, let's clearly define what you are worried about.

WHAT LATE RENT MEANS TO THE LANDLORD

There are really three questions that most landlords have when the rent is late (and the tenant has not called to explain):

1. Will it cause me to miss my own payments for mortgage, insurance, and/or utilities?
2. Will this rent be late again next month and the month after? Is the tenant going to refuse to pay altogether and cause me real grief?
3. If it's the first late rent payment from a good payer, how do I handle this without offending and potentially losing the good tenant?

It's important to understand that when the rent is late, most landlords, particularly those new to the game, experience two emotions: fear and anger. You're afraid because the late rent threatens your ownership of the property. In most cases landlords have a very thin margin. You are probably counting on that rent to make a hefty mortgage payment. Without the rent, you'll have to come up with the money elsewhere and that can

121

cause you serious difficulty. And, you're angry at the tenant for putting you in this position.

What's important to remember is that the tenant is also probably experiencing fear and anger. The tenant is probably afraid of what will happen because of the late rent. In the case of most tenants (we'll talk about "professional tenant" problems later), they don't know what you can or will do. They're worried about their credit standing and the roof over their heads. And, they are often angry at themselves for letting this situation occur.

If you allow your emotions to rule and respond in a fearful or angry way, chances are you will provoke a similar response from the tenant. You could actually turn a harmless situation of a payment lost in the mail into a serious problem that could mean really late rent, a lost tenant, or worse.

Hint: What's worse than a tenant who moves without paying? You're a new landlord if you ask that. The answer is a tenant who stays and won't pay!

HOW TO PROCEED

It's important at the onset to control your emotions. If the rent is late, it's a business problem and needs to be dealt with accordingly. You should proceed in the following manner:

Before taking any action you must determine why the rent is late. There are many, many reasons from the simple and innocuous to the difficult and underhanded. You can't know what to do until you figure out what the problem really is. In case you're scratching your head trying to figure it out, here's a list of some possible causes for late rent:

- *It's in the mail.* Yes, once in a great while a rent check really does get lost in the mail—though not too often!
- *The tenant forgot.* Incredible, isn't it? How can anyone forget to pay the rent? But it happens.
- *There's a problem with the house and the tenant is purposely holding back the rent until you fix it.* You should know about this already from earlier conversations with the tenant.

- *The tenants don't have the money because a check they are expecting is late.* That's their problem, right? Except now they're making it yours.
- *The tenant lost his or her job and just doesn't have the money.*
- *The tenant is sick, can't work, can't even get out of bed to call you.* It helps if you're a doctor. If not, you could have a problem.
- *The tenant won't pay and won't give a reason.* You do have a serious problem.

How do you know if the problem is easy or difficult? You talk to the tenant. You can never define the problem yourself. You can only figure it out through communications.

Hint: What's a landlord in who never goes out to talk to his or her tenants? The answer? In foreclosure!

When the rent is late, I always make it a point to drop by to see the tenant. If it's a tenant who has previously paid well and who pays through the mail, I might wait as long as three days before dropping by. For a really good tenant, I might just call up and say, "By the way, the rent payment hasn't arrived. Is there a problem?" Chances are this tenant will be surprised, say they mailed it a week ago and they'll be happy to cancel the check and give me a cashier's check or even cash if I want it. I then

L A N D L O R D ' S   S T O R Y

Sometimes, you just have to accept late rent. I once had a tenant who depended on her Social Security check to pay the rent. She was always five days late. The reason? Her Social Security check arrived on the fifth of the month.

I had a choice. I could rant and rave and demand that payment be made on the first, in which case it would still arrive on the fifth. Or I could accept the fact that she would always be punctually five days late. She was a good tenant, always paid late, promptly, and I never said a word. She stayed for nearly seven years, and never complained about anything, even once. One of the best tenants I ever had.

drop by and pick up the rent. There are no hard feelings. I haven't lost a good tenant. And my worries are assuaged.

LOCATING THE TENANT

When the rent is late, your first task is to find the tenant, and determine why and what the tenant intends to do about it.

Finding the tenant is usually easy. When I'm looking, I just come by at dinner time. Most tenants are at home.

Sometimes, however, the tenant isn't home. They aren't home when you come by at dinner time, in the morning, or the afternoon. You come back several times and the tenant still isn't around. It's easy to become aggravated, frustrated—even hostile—and lose your perspective. Now, even if it's all innocent, you visualize a plot and overreact.

Who knows? It could have been a family emergency—perhaps a son or daughter was injured in an auto accident or a distant parent took desperately ill. In times like those, most of us forget the mundane things, like rent, and just react to the immediate need.

First of all, call the tenant. They may have call forwarding on their phone or at least an answering machine. If you don't get them, at least leave an urgent message.

Next, if you still can't reach them, go back to the rental agreement. If you've got a good rental agreement and application, they will list a couple of phone numbers of relatives. Give them a call. After all, you have a legitimate concern—your rent. Find out if something happened to the family. If it is an emergency and it's a good tenant, be especially nice. Let the person you call know you're concerned. Ask them to have the tenant call you and let them know that if they need time, you'll work something out. Chances are you'll get a call back within a few hours and the rent check the next day.

If the relative phone calls don't work out, then it's time to become a snoop. Go around and talk to the neighbors. It's positively amazing what neighbors know. Tell the neighbors you own the property, you can't find the tenants and you're worried that something might be amiss. Chances are if the neighbors know anything, they'll dump it right on you. Maybe instead of an emergency, there are marital troubles. There was a terrible

I had a very good tenant who stayed in my property for more than two years. Then one day, the rent was late. I called, but there was no answer. I came by and the front door was locked and nobody was home. I talked to the neighbors and they said that the night before my tenants had packed up their belongings in a rental truck and left.

I rechecked the property and found the back door unlocked and the house dirty, but empty. They had abandoned it.

I was okay with this. They hadn't cost me any lost rent. I still had the security deposit to take care of cleaning and I could reclaim my house. Yes, I would have preferred a more orderly termination, but given the alternative of what they could have done (stayed, not paid, and ruined the house), I was not going to complain.

fight and they split—husband in one direction, wife in the other. Or the tenant got laid off work and just packed up and took off.

In a worst-case scenario where you can't find the tenant, and the relatives and neighbors aren't helpful, leave a card on the front door saying you were there and keep coming back. Hopefully, sooner or later they will turn up. If they don't, you may have to start unlawful detainer action (see the chapter on eviction), but that's particularly hard if the tenants simply aren't there.

But take heart—in years of being a landlord, only once did tenants leave all their furniture and bug out on me and that was a long time ago. Usually, they're there, even if just hiding out and pretending not to be home.

WHY IS THE RENT LATE?

Remember, your first goal is to find out why. Only after you've found out what the problem is can you take appropriate action. You're there first and foremost to listen.

Okay, the rent's late, you've found the tenant and you've listened. Now what? Assuming the problem isn't something simple like the rent simply being lost in the mail, you now have to decide what to do. We'll discuss what action you should take in the next chapter. First, however, here are a couple of side issues to help you be sure the rent isn't late in the future.

GETTING PAID

Mailing versus Picking Up the Rent

Should you have the tenant mail the check to you or should you go out and pick it up personally? The answer, of course, depends entirely on the tenant. In my experience I have found that most often tenants in low-rent properties expect the landlord to come by on rent day and collect payment. If you don't come by, they don't pay.

Middle-rent to upper-rent properties, on the other hand, often attract tenants who would think you absurd if not a little paranoid if you came by to collect the rent monthly. They assume they will send it in along with the utility, phone, and other bills.

I have done it both ways and can assure you that getting the rent check in the mail is by far the easier method, when it arrives. In either case, however, if the rent is late you must contact the tenant and do it quickly.

If you are having the rent sent to you, one technique that some landlords use successfully is to mail the tenant a postage paid envelope around the middle of the month. All the tenant has to do then is put the check in and drop it in the mail box. This simple device is quite inexpensive and can save a lot of late payments.

Hint: You may be able to establish a direct deposit system for your tenants. Your tenants must set it up with their banks. On the specified day of the month, the rent money will automatically be deducted from their checking accounts and electronically deposited to your account. The system can be set up with an alert given to you if there's insufficient funds in a tenant's account to make the transfer.

Beware of Partial Rent Payments

Many times tenants will say that they can't pay the entire month's rent, but they can pay a week's worth, or two weeks' worth. They offer to give you the partial payment and pay the remainder at the end of that time.

Most landlords feel that a tenant in the rental is worth twelve in the bush. Better to take the short payment and worry about the rest later. Well, yes and no. If it's good tenants in a bad spot who just need a little help, you're probably safe in taking the partial rent. However, if you're renting on a month-to-month tenancy, an unscrupulous tenant can now say that by accepting partial payment, you've changed the terms of the rental arrangement. You've now agreed to accept rent weekly, instead of monthly. (Many areas have very different laws regulating weekly rentals.)

Further, if this is a tenant who has repeatedly given you trouble and you begin eviction proceedings and then accept a partial rent payment, you have, in effect, called off the eviction. If the tenant subsequently doesn't pay any more, in most locales you must start all over again with the first notice. You could have lost many weeks of your most precious asset—time.

IF THE CHECK BOUNCES

Sometimes the rent check will bounce. What do you do?

If the tenant has a reasonable explanation, quickly makes the check good, and promises it will never happen again, it's usually better to forgive and (sort of) forget.

However, if the check ever bounces again, then insist that from that point on that tenant pay you with cash, a cashier's check, or a money order instead of a personal check. You simply have to say you can't be bothered with the delays and inconveniences of bounced checks. If the tenant wants to continue on, he or she must pay in cash or cash equivalent.

As an aside, any rent check that I get in the mail I deposit *immediately,* the same day if possible. I also have an arrangement with my bank that any check that does not clear results in an *immediate* phone call notifying me of the problem. I don't wait the three to five days it takes for the bank to send out a letter. Thus, I usually know within two days when a rent check doesn't clear the tenant's bank. What do I do then?

I go to my bank, pick up the check stamped not paid because of "insufficient funds," and take the check to go see my tenant.

I inform the tenant that not only is the rent late, but now I've been given a bad check. The criminal penalties for issuing a bad check vary from one area of the country to another, but are getting increasingly severe. I know what the penalties are in my area and I mention these.

I am willing to accept payment in cash in exchange for the bad check. I will also take a money order and, if they are legitimate, traveler's checks.

I will not take another personal check, although I will accept a cashier's check. (Note: Within the last few years banks have sometimes weaseled out of honoring cashier's checks, sometimes even their own, depending on the circumstances.)

If the tenant cannot or will not give me cash or cash equivalent for the bad check, I serve the first eviction notice in the eviction process. (I also hang onto the bad check—it can prove helpful if the matter ever gets to a court hearing.)

THE BOTTOM LINE

Don't ever let late rent slip by. The rent is your due for providing housing to the tenant. Every day that it goes unpaid means that you are providing free housing. Further, unpaid rent means that your financial security and even ownership of your property are being threatened. Don't forget the domino effect in apartment buildings: if one tenant doesn't pay and brags about getting away with it, expect the same from other tenants.

CHAPTER 14

When the Tenant Won't Pay and Won't Move

The rent is late; you've gone out to see the tenants; you still don't have the money. Now, what do you do?

Hint: If the tenant repeatedly insists that the check was lost in the mail, don't argue. Just agree and say you want another check—cashier's this time—or cash, immediately. The lost check can be cancelled or you'll return it whenever it shows up. That should end that line of argument by the tenant.

WHEN THE TENANT "CAN'T" PAY

The most common reason that a tenant will give for not paying the rent (after you've cleared up the business about it being lost in the mail) is that they don't have the money right now. There's been an unfortunate delay. The tenant's boss didn't get the paychecks out that week or the money they were expecting from Aunt Bertha simply hasn't shown up. The tenant wants to pay, but explains they simply can't right now. If you're just willing to wait awhile, a few days, perhaps a week or two, they'll get the money to you.

Should you wait?

No one wants to be unkind, but it's important to remember that renting property is a business just like any other. How long do you think a gas station owner, for example, would stay in business if he gave out free gas to everyone who stopped by and said their tank was empty and that they didn't have any money?

The tenants obviously have a problem, but they want to take their problem and make it yours. Their problem is that they can't pay the rent right now. It's their responsibility to find a solution. That solution has to be either they get the money from somewhere or move out.

If, however, you agree to allow them not to pay even for a short while such as a week or two, now it's your problem. You have a nonpaying tenant. What are you going to do about it?

> **Hint:** What is the only acceptable answer a tenant can give for late rent? Answer? "Sorry I'm late. Here's the rent, in cash."

DEMANDING THE RENT

Whatever you do, don't let the tenant put you off. Experienced landlords know that in almost all cases tenants can come up with the money if they feel they have to. People usually have money in a savings account or they can borrow from relatives. But they hesitate to seek funds from such a source unless it's an emergency, and often they don't define late rent as an emergency.

You need to convince your tenants to reprioritize their financial decisions. It's important that they see that the rent must be paid first. You don't want it at the end of a long list of other bills.

You can be sympathetic, but you also must make it clear that the rent has to be paid—and paid on time. Perhaps you might say something such as, "I'm sorry to hear that _____ (fill in the blank with the tenant's problem), but you must know that the rent comes first. You have to have a roof over your head. So, I've made a special trip to collect it. I'm here for the rent."

Once you make it clear that you are there for the rent and will not be moved until it's paid, they will often come up with it. They will also come to understand that you are someone who will not be put off, and they will think twice next month about putting you at the end of their list of people to be paid.

Demand the rent you are entitled to and most of the time you will get it. On the other hand, while it's important to be a "no nonsense" landlord, do not be mean, vindictive, loud, insulting, or overbearing. Always speak quietly and calmly, but firmly. The rent is due. You're here to pick it up. You accept no excuses.

THE TENANT WON'T PAY

On the other hand, the tenant simply may not be able or willing to pay. You must dig deeper to find out why.

Is the breadwinner out of work? Was there an emergency (someone got into a car accident)? Did the money get spent elsewhere? Is the rent simply too high?

It may be time to reason with the tenant. If the rent is simply too high or they are in an impossible financial situation, you may want to suggest that the tenant consider moving to a lower-cost rental or even to a relative's home, until things get better. You can point out that this will save the tenant's credit reputation and will convert them from being in an impossible rental situation to one which they can handle. You may even want to use some of their security deposit to facilitate this. Remember, quickly getting rid of a tenant who can't pay is far better than having them stay while you try to collect rent in court.

I have even chipped in to help pay for movers to get a tenant who couldn't pay out of the property. Remember, you can't squeeze blood from a turnip or get money out of an empty wallet. If they just don't have the money, then your best solution is to find an amicable way for them to move somewhere else.

On the other hand, if the excuse is implausible or they are adamant about staying or they refuse to work with you, you're probably in a situation that's only going to get worse. If that's the case, you're probably dealing with a tenant who will simply drag the matter out, wasting your time and not ever paying. You will probably be best off to serve this tenant immediately with a notice to pay or quit (the first step in an eviction). (See Chapter 15 on evictions.)

Sometimes serving the eviction notice results in your getting your rent paid—if not immediately, within a day or two. If this tenant does pay up, however, I would make it perfectly clear to them that in the future you expect the rent to continue to be paid on time, else that eviction notice will be back.

Hint: You want to keep the tenants, so you're afraid to begin eviction for fear of offending them. It's true—you could lose a tenant by serving the first eviction notice. On the other hand, you may lose the tenant anyway and the sooner you begin eviction, the sooner a nonpaying tenant will get out and you'll be able to rent to someone who will pay.

THE ONE-TIME PROBLEM

In rare cases, you may find that a tenant is late in paying the rent, but you're sure that the tenant will eventually pay and *that this is only a one-time problem.* If the tenants are responsible (they call you before you call them) and explain a one-time extenuating circumstance, you may want to allow them time to get the rent together. But be careful. If in the end they don't pay up, each day's delay is another day's rent lost, probably forever. Be absolutely sure you and your tenants agree on the final date when the rent is due and that there's a *penalty* included for the late payment. The penalty rams home the fact that late payment is not without consequences.

LANDLORD'S STORY

I once had an excellent tenant who lived with her son, an airline pilot. She depended on her son's paycheck for the rent. One month he was in Saudi Arabia and his company sent his check to him there instead of to the house. She had to wait until he got back, nearly three weeks, before it could be straightened out. However, she did not simply let things hang. She called me the day the rent was due and explained the situation. I agreed to wait and three weeks later, I got full payment.

THE "SOFTY" LANDLORD

A first-time landlord may feel sorry for his or her tenants' difficulties. A tenant may be out of work, sick, may have lost his or her wallet, or whatever. You are a human being and you feel sorry for the tenant's troubles. You want to help them out and, unfortunately for you, the means to help them is oh so obvious and easy; you can just allow them to pay late. Just a few days late at first, then a week, then two, then maybe a month. It will help them out so much.

If you decide to operate your property as a charitable venture, that's fine. Just be sure that you know what you're doing up front and that you're prepared for the consequences, such as not being able to make your own mortgage, tax, and insurance payments.

If you don't want to end up a pauper yourself, you'll very quickly realize that not only your profits, but your financial survival require that you see yourself strictly as a businessperson.

If you simply can't overlook the plight of the helpless and the poor (who just happen to be occupying your house), then I suggest you get out of the rental business at once. You will not only lose money but you may even end up doing a disservice to those who come to you for help by inadvertently conspiring to lead them further into debt.

TENANTS ARE TOUGH

As a landlord, always remember that tenants are constantly sizing you up. If you look like a soft touch, you'll find that even the ones who pay regularly begin appealing to your sympathies. It may not be late rent; it could be repainting the premises in colors they prefer . . . or putting in new carpeting . . . or even reducing the rent.

Further, problem tenants, particularly those who have survived the threats and feeble actions of other less adroit landlords, can become quite skilled at taking advantage. They probe with late rent payments, with unreasonable demands, even with threats to sue you if you don't comply with their wishes. They are looking for softness and if they find it in you, you can be sure they will take full advantage of it.

If you let them, some tenants will put the rent payment last, after the car payment, clothing, bowling, eating out, or whatever. They may stop keeping up the property. They may leave it a mess. Certainly not every tenant, not even most tenants will do this. But there are enough who will to change your hair from whatever color it now is to gray.

THE LANDLORD'S GUIDELINES FOR RENT COLLECTION

Here are some guidelines that you should post next to the phone you use for making and receiving rents:

Rules for Collecting Rent

- The rent must always be paid.
- Whatever you give away in rent to the tenant, you probably will never get back.
- There are no acceptable excuses for late rent.

Good tenants expect a landlord to act like one: businesslike and professional. I've been both a landlord and a tenant. When I was a tenant, I paid my rent on time. If I didn't, I fully expected the landlord to come around asking for it and would acknowledge that he had every right to demand it from me. If I couldn't pay or refused or simply spent the money elsewhere, I wouldn't blame the landlord a bit for giving me an eviction notice. I would deserve it! In fact, if the landlord overlooked my lateness or refusal to pay, I would have every right to think him a fool.

A WORD ABOUT RECEIPTS

When the tenants pay up, give them a receipt. They're entitled to one both morally and legally. Be sure, however, that the receipt specifies the time period for which the rent was paid. Putting in the exact time period, for example, June 1 through June 30 (with the year), avoids later confusion and argument.

If you receive partial payment (for example, two weeks' worth), indicate the dates that the partial payment covers. Otherwise if you later are forced to proceed with eviction, the tenant may claim that the partial payment was intended to cover the whole month, and then your eviction proceedings may be delayed.

YOU'RE A LANDLORD—BE PROUD OF IT

As a landlord, it is your job to collect rent, especially when it's late. If you do it fairly both to yourself and to your tenants, you will find that not only do you prosper, but your tenants respect you and in most cases pay promptly.

Eviction

Eviction is usually a last resort. The tenant won't pay the rent and won't vacate the premises. You're losing time, money, and patience. You've talked with the tenant. You've served notices. Nothing has worked. Now it's time to consider evicting the tenant.

Hint: Sometimes you will want to evict a tenant for a reason other than nonpayment of rent. For example, they could be breaking a term of their rental agreement, such as having too many people in the premises or having loud parties late at night. Or you may want to terminate the tenancy (in accordance with the rental agreement) in order to use the property for other purposes. Tenants often contest this last kind of eviction (discussed later in this chapter).

The eviction process is fairly straightforward and quick in almost all areas of the country. When you seek an eviction, you usually have priority in terms of court time and often you can get a judgment and the eviction in a matter of a few weeks or so. (But not always, as we'll soon see.)

Experienced landlords know the eviction process quite well, but may pick up a few ideas they hadn't considered in this chapter. For those who have not yet or are just now going through their first eviction, read closely.

DO YOU NEED AN ATTORNEY?

The answer is absolutely "yes," the first time. After that, you will see how it's done and will probably want to try it yourself. Most experienced landlords handle their own court evictions and as long as everything goes according to plan, have little trouble doing this.

The biggest question for the new landlord often is, how do you find a good eviction attorney? I suggest that you check with local property managers and real estate agents who handle rentals. Usually there are attorneys nearby who do nothing but handle evictions. That's their bread and butter. They know all the nuances of the local laws, they know the judges, they know from vast experience what's going to happen and how long it's likely to take. And they also usually have set fees.

Sometimes these fees may seem excessive, particularly when you learn how little work is actually involved. However, it's best to learn from an expert and my feeling is that their fees are usually worth it. You should learn enough to be able to handle it yourself in the future.

THE EVICTION PROCESS

The actual eviction process is straightforward. Below are the steps usually taken. Keep in mind that each state has different laws for eviction, which means that time limits and required document filings will differ.

1. Serve the initial pay-or-quit notice (3-day, 5-day, or according to local statute).
2. File the unlawful detainer (eviction) action papers.
3. Serve the eviction papers.
4. Show up as scheduled in appropriate court for hearing.
5. Tell your story to the judge and, if the tenants do not show, get a judgment to collect the monies owed to you and an eviction.
6. Have final eviction papers, with the date of eviction, served on the tenants.
7. Have the appropriate law enforcement agency evict the tenants on the date. If it gets this far, you will probably have to pay for a local moving company to come and take the tenants' belongings and have them put into storage for later disposition.
8. Have the law enforcement present give possession of the property back to you.

The total time in an uncontested eviction shouldn't be much more than four to eight weeks with six weeks being about average. Of course, if the eviction is contested, then all bets are off. We'll discuss this later, but first let's consider what many landlords would really like to do with tenants who won't pay and won't "quit" (leave the property).

SELF-HELP EVICTIONS

What should be obvious from the eviction procedure outlined above is that it takes time and you lose around six weeks' worth of rent in an

LANDLORD'S STORY

A number of years ago, Hal was having a lot of trouble with some tenants in a house he owned. First they were late with the rent. Then they stopped paying altogether. Finally, they wouldn't answer their phone when he called.

Hal was getting frustrated and decided to kick the tenants out. However, when he heard that a local attorney wanted a thousand dollars to handle the eviction for him, he scoffed and said he would do it himself.

It was the dead of winter and nights typically dropped well below freezing. Hal showed up one morning at the house and banged on the door until the tenants finally answered. He told them he wanted them out by that afternoon. If they weren't out, he was going to come around with a hammer and break all the windows. (He figured he could get the windows replaced for a lot less than paying an attorney.)

The tenants said that was against the law. If he did that, they would call the sheriff. Hal said they could indeed call the sheriff if they wanted, but by then the windows would be all gone and they'd be sleeping in the cold.

Needless to say, Hal impressed the tenants as being something of a madman and sure enough, they were out by that evening. Hal congratulated himself on a job well done.

Of course, Hal was just very lucky. If the tenants had been savvy, they might have sued him for threatening them. If they were really savvy, they might have simply stayed and waited. If he carried out his threat, they could have said that perhaps one of their children had been injured on broken glass; perhaps their furniture had been damaged by rain coming in the broken windows. Perhaps someone had come in and robbed them while the windows were gone. Before the tenants were done, they might have ended up owning the property and Hal could have been a tenant himself somewhere else.

uncontested eviction. And it's costly. You have some court costs to pay, you have to pay an attorney (at least the first time out), and you conceivably could have to pay a moving company to collect and store the tenants' furniture. Wouldn't it simply be much easier to just get a bunch of your burly friends, show up one night, and throw the tenants out? Simpler? Yes. Legal? No.

I mention the above tale first because it's absolutely true and second because it illustrates about the stupidest thing a landlord can do. The last thing you want is to put yourself in a position where a tenant has good grounds for suing you. In today's litigious society, you can be fairly sure that if you try any sort of self-help eviction, you will get caught and it will be costly!

Here's a partial list of some self-help actions that you *do not* want to do:

- *Do not* break the windows on the house, remove the doors, or anything else that makes the premises uninhabitable.
- *Do not* turn off the utilities (water, gas, electric, etc.) or plug up the sewer or septic system.
- *Do not* padlock the tenants out of the property.
- *Do not* harm their pets or leave gates open so the pets can run loose.
- *Do not* threaten the tenants.
- *Do not* disturb their right to "quiet enjoyment" of the property.
- *Do not* do anything else that would give the tenants cause to sue you.

Although it might still be condoned in backwoods areas, I personally know of no part of the country that still allows self-help evictions. You want the tenants out, you go to court.

SERVING NOTICES

Earlier in this chapter we went through a typical procedure for the legal eviction of tenants. Let's go back now and dwell a bit longer on one aspect of that—serving notices.

The Pay-or-Quit Notice

In almost all areas you must begin the eviction process by serving a pay-or-quit notice. The purpose of this notice is to give tenants written notice that either they must pay the full amount of rent then owed, or they must quit the premises within a specified period of time. The period varies according to state. In Illinois, for example, it's five days and a 5-day notice is used. In California it's a 3-day notice and tenants have three days to get out or pay.

Only after you have served this notice and tenants have not paid and not quit can you go to court to commence the actual eviction proceeding, usually called an "unlawful detainer" action.

The pay-or-quit notice is usually presented by a landlord directly to a tenant. Most landlords use it sparingly because it's sure to alienate a tenant. Some use it to get faltering tenants back on track; to let them know the landlord really does mean business. A few landlords use these too frequently and offend an otherwise good tenant who subsequently leaves.

Used sparingly and only when absolutely necessary, the notice can be very effective in spurring a delinquent tenant into performing. Used indiscriminately, it can anger good tenants and result in excessive move-outs. (See the appendix for a sample notice.)

The notice itself does not have to be in any special form, although it should have the following items on it:

- Address of the rental
- Correct names of the tenants
- The total amount due and what period of time this covers
- The time to pay it (you can give them more time, if you want—the state only sets the minimum time you must give)
- The date
- Your signature

The Notice to Quit

A variation of the pay-or-quit notice is a similar document that does not give a monetary amount. This is used when the tenant has not paid the rent, but refuses to quit after you have given proper notice asking them to move out. Everything else is essentially the same—only there is no dollar figure on the notice.

HAVING THE SHERIFF SERVE NOTICES

After you've served initial notice and the tenants have not quit or paid up the rent, there are now other notices to be served. The number and purpose vary according to your area, but there will be at least two: (1) the initial notice of eviction and (2) the later court-order notice that the tenants must move. There may be intermediate steps as well.

You can serve these notices yourself. However, a better way is to have the local police department or sheriff's office serve the notice. They will do this for what is usually a small fee.

The importance of this, of course, is that when the tenants see the cops coming to the door, they are likely to be far more impressed than when they see you coming to the door. A few dollars spent here might be just enough to get the tenants to move on their own, allowing you to avoid having to follow through on the entire eviction.

KEEP YOUR EYE ON THE GOAL

This brings us back to the primary goal—getting the tenants out. If you're a typical landlord, you're usually not all that interested in going through the entire eviction process. If you can just get the tenants out (or the back rent paid) before it gets to the judge, you can save yourself considerable money in filing fees, attorney's costs, and additional lost rent.

Hint: Sometimes tenants will play brinkmanship, repeatedly taking you right to the edge before paying. In that case you may simply want to terminate the tenancy because the hassle of having them as tenants probably won't be worthwhile to you.

An exception here is if the tenants have assets. If they do, you may want to proceed to get a judgment against them in the hopes of collecting back rent and costs later on down the road.

In most cases, however, tenants who fail to pay rent are "judgment proof" because they don't have any assets you can attach. In this case, just getting them out quickly, as noted above, is usually your best bet.

MOST TENANTS WILL MOVE FIRST

Most tenants will simply roll over and play dead when you threaten eviction. They know they haven't paid the rent. They know they are in the wrong. They feel guilty. They act guilty. They are just trying to stall and gain some time.

I can recall less than a handful of situations in decades of being a landlord and being involved with other landlords where the tenants actually stayed right to the bitter end and the sheriff had to come and move them out. After all, that's tantamount to having your possessions taken away from you, perhaps never to be seen again. (The tenants can, of course, regain their possessions by paying storage and other costs.) Most sane tenants will move before the eviction date.

Sometimes, however (particularly if there's a nasty divorce involved), the tenants will be unable to act. They will be arguing between themselves even as they are physically evicted.

> **Hint:** In my experience, most judges won't grant you an unlawful detainer until all the money you hold, meaning the security deposit, has been applied to the rent. That means that if you hold a month's security deposit, it will be at least 30 days after the tenant stopped paying rent before the judge is likely to act.

TENANTS WHO CONTEST THE EVICTION

Thus far we have been discussing an eviction that the tenants do not contest. In some cases, however, savvy tenants will appear in court before the judge and contest the eviction.

If you're a new landlord, you'll be asking yourself, "On what grounds can the tenants possibly contest eviction if they haven't paid their rent?" The answer is that at the least they can claim hardship. At the worst, they can claim that you've done something to them that caused them not to pay rent and that you're to blame.

L A N D L O R D ' S   S T O R Y

Sally rented an apartment to a family with two small children. After staying there nearly six months, they stopped paying rent and refused to move. Nothing she could say or do would change their actions. So she tried eviction.

At the court proceedings, the tenants showed up with their small children. They claimed they had both lost their jobs and were looking for work. They just needed more time. They were particularly worried about their children missing school if they were evicted. Besides, they said they had nowhere to go. The judge gave them a month to come up with the money they owed.

A month later they were back in court. The children were crying, the mother was crying, the father was choked with emotion. They had tried, but they needed more time. The judge gave them another month.

It happened three times for a total of three months. At the end of the third month, they just didn't show and the judge finally ordered the eviction, to take place in three weeks.

Sally served all the papers, of course, but they didn't move . . . until the day before the sheriff showed up along with the moving van Sally had paid for. They were suddenly gone, leaving the property a mess.

Altogether, they were able to stay in the property for four-and-a-half months without paying rent. Because they were "judgment proof," Sally had no real chance of recovering any of her costs.

If you want to learn what could happen in a worst-case scenario, I suggest you rent the video "Pacific Heights." I found the movie, though not aesthetically pleasing, absolutely mesmerizing in terms of its portrayal of a "tenant from hell." In the movie, an unscrupulous tenant rents an apartment with the specific goal of ruining the owners/landlords so that he can take over the building after they cannot afford the mortgage payments and lose the property to foreclosure. Need more be said?

A CAUTION REGARDING PARTIAL PAYMENTS

After you begin the eviction process, a tenant may come to you with a partial payment. For example, the tenant may owe five weeks' rent. She may say she doesn't have the full amount, but she has one week's rent.

She wants to give it to you as evidence of her good intentions to pay the rest.

Most beginning landlords will take the money on the assumption that one in the hand is worth five in the bush. At least you've got some cash.

The problem is that accepting any money at all in partial payment from the tenant may corrupt the eviction process. In other words, once you've accepted a partial payment, if you want to evict the tenant, you may have to start all over again from the beginning with all of the notices. Accepting one week's part payment, in this example, could have the effect of setting you back a month or more in the eviction process. Be sure to check with an attorney in your state to see what local policy is regarding the acceptance of partial rental payment during an eviction.

AFTER THE EVICTION

Along with the eviction, you will normally also get a judgment from the court for your costs. You can now attempt to trace the former tenants, garnish wages, attach bank accounts, and so forth. It's actually a fascinating process, if you have the time and the gumption for it.

A simpler method, and one that often nets better results, is to turn the whole mess over to a collection agency. The agency usually has far more resources than you can muster and probably has both a better chance of tracking down the former tenant as well as getting the cash.

Be aware, however, that most collection agencies work on a percentage basis. So while they may recover the funds, they may keep a third or more for their efforts, depending on the difficulty of getting payment and your contract with them. Nevertheless, a part of the otherwise lost funds is better than none at all. Collection agencies can be found under that heading in the yellow pages of the phone book.

AFTER YOU GET THE PROPERTY BACK

As soon as the tenants are evicted, secure the premises. That means new door locks throughout as well as locks on all windows. Immediately begin refurbishing work, particularly on the exterior. Make it quite apparent that someone is taking care of the property. Also, if it's a single family house, get someone to frequently check on the premises, at least for the first few days. A rental, particularly a separate property, left vacant after an eviction is a prime target for vandals. A lesser danger is that the former tenants, angered by the eviction, might come back and attempt to do damage to the property. In most cases, however, such tenants are long gone.

Eviction should be a last resort. But when you use it, move quickly and forcefully.

When the Tenant Abandons the Property

The tenant who abandons the rental may, at the time, seem like a real headache to you. However, in actuality it's probably a gift. After all, with the property abandoned, you can get in there, clean it up, and rent it. (What's far worse is the tenant who won't pay and won't leave! See Chapter 14.)

There are several different scenarios that can happen with abandonment, each with its own problems and solutions. We'll consider several here.

WHEN THE TENANT WHO IS BEHIND IN RENT ABANDONS

If you've been a landlord for any time at all, you've run into this situation. Your tenant, for whatever reason, isn't paying rent. A week or two goes by and you're getting increasingly frustrated. You've stopped by many times, but the tenant just won't, or can't, pay. You're calculating how much of the security deposit is left, after applying it toward the unpaid rent, and it's quickly working its way down to zero. You're angry and frustrated and wondering if you'll have to go to a formal eviction.

Suddenly one day when you show up to argue with the tenant, you find the door is wide open. You peek in and discover that the tenant and all the furniture are gone. The tenant has abandoned the property. What do you do? Whoop for joy! You've just been saved the cost and hassle of an eviction.

Get someone else to go in with you (to be able to later swear that you didn't take any of the tenant's possessions that might have been there) and check out the premises. If it's truly empty, go back to the rental agreement and call every reference listed there. Chances are I'd discover the tenant had moved elsewhere. Maybe they even left the key for me with a neighbor. Then I'd quickly change the locks, get a crew in there to clean it up and find a new tenant. I'd do this as quickly as possible to save rental time.

The only real problem with this course of action is that the tenant never gave me back the key. And until that happens, technically, the tenant still has rights to the property. However, I suspect it would be difficult, in the situation described above, for anyone to contend that the tenant intended to continue living there.

It's a different situation when part of the furniture is gone and part remains. I've known landlords who stayed in front of a property at night waiting for tenants to show up who were clandestinely moving out. When they appeared, long after midnight, the landlord would demand to know what was going on.

Usually the tenants sheepishly admit they don't have the rent and are skipping out. The landlord can then explain the consequences of such action and ask them to sign a statement that they were abandoning the property as of the next day and to give up the keys, which they usually will do.

WHEN THE TENANT ABANDONS, BUT LEAVES BEHIND FURNITURE

A much trickier situation is when the tenant isn't paying rent and isn't at the property. But the furniture remains there.

As long as there's furniture in the rental, you can't assume abandonment. My suggestion is that if a situation such as noted following occurs, you go back to that rental application where you asked for the names of relatives or close friends and start calling. Also check with the bank or any other source that may have heard from your tenant. Chances are someone will know where they are and you can make contact.

LANDLORD'S STORY

A good number of years ago (when things were done more informally), a young friend of mine, Tony, was renting apartments. One tenant was behind in his rent and whenever Tony went to check up, that tenant wasn't there. But, obviously, the furniture was. (Tony used a master key to get in to check.)

Weeks went by, then a month. Tony talked to the neighbors, but they couldn't shed light on the situation. Finally, after a month, Tony decided the tenants had abandoned the apartment. He had the choice of going through the cost of a formal eviction, or just deciding on his own that the tenants had moved out and would never be back. He thought about it and just decided they had left.

So, he called in movers and had the tenants' furniture moved out. Then he cleaned up the apartment and rented it. A few weeks later, he sold the furniture to an auction company.

Imagine Tony's surprise when a week after that, the tenants showed up, angry as can be, wondering what happened to their apartment and furniture! It turned out they had gone on vacation and mailed the rent check in. However, they had addressed it incorrectly and it never arrived. And they were a couple of weeks late getting back.

Needless to say, Tony was red-faced. Ultimately, to keep the tenants from suing him, he had to give them a different rental unit, including a month's free rent, and pay for new furniture!

All of which is to say, never assume abandonment, no matter how things look. And when taking any action, be sure you're on solid legal footing.

If you can't make contact, you will probably have to get an unlawful detainer action before you can remove the furniture. Yes, it's costly and perhaps it might be seen as a waste of time. On the other hand, trying self-help, as described above, can be even more costly and time consuming.

THE TENANT WHO DIES IN THE PROPERTY

Life goes on and life ends. Sometimes tenants will die in your property. If that happens, what do you do?

I'm not sure there are any pat answers; however, here are my suggestions. First, be sure that someone in fact did die. I knew of a landlord who would go into an apartment at the drop of a hat, convinced the tenant had died. If the tenant's cat was meowing for a few days, if the rent was a bit late, if she didn't see the tenant three mornings in a row, in she went to check. (Remember, you should have included in your rental agreement the right to reasonable entry to the property in the event of an emergency.) The trouble was, the tenant never died. Usually the tenant was away on a trip, or sleeping late, or some such thing.

Sometimes, however, there's not such a nice result. Sometimes, the tenant does die. A cat meowing for days, no rent payment, sometimes even a smell, can alert you that there's potentially a big problem.

Exercise your right to inspect the property in an emergency. This may mean calling and banging on the door. If repeated attempts fail to gain anyone's attention, go back to your application and see whom to call in an emergency and call that person.

If all else fails, and if you believe it truly is an emergency, then go inside, presumably with another person to be able to verify that you didn't take or damage anything.

If you find what you believe to be a dead body, stop. Do not proceed. Immediately call 911 or the fire department and report what you believe you've seen. Remember, a person isn't dead until pronounced so by a doctor or medical examiner.

Do not touch anything in the rental nor let anyone else touch anything. At this time you have no idea if the person died of natural causes or if it was a murder. Your apartment may become a crime scene and the police will be gratified to learn that you didn't mess it up.

Get on the phone and call the tenant's relatives or friends (whose names you get from the application). Try to locate and notify the next of kin. Be as gentle as possible. After all, you may be letting someone know that a loved one has died.

Once the medical examiner has determined that the death was from natural causes (which is probably going to be the case), let the next of kin in to remove the body to a mortuary for burial. Also, you may want to allow them to take a suit or a dress as needed for the funeral.

There now only remains the matter of the tenant's furniture and personal possessions. Usually fairly quickly someone will be appointed to take care of the estate, either an administrator (court appointed) or executor (designated by the deceased). This person will want you to release the possessions. Be sure that the person is, indeed, entitled to handle the estate. Typically this person will be able to produce court-approved documents to that effect. If you're not sure about them, take them to a lawyer or call the court.

On the other hand, if the tenant had few and modest possessions, the relatives may simply not want to bother with the cost and hassle of a probate, but may instead simply want to divide up and sell what's there. Technically this should not be done, but as a practical matter, it's done all the time. You can only use your best judgment here.

Because it is common practice to pay off the deceased person's debts from his or her estate, be sure that you put in your bill for all unpaid rent. This includes not only back rent until the tenant died, but also any time that the tenant's possessions are in the property and you can't rerent. If there's a sizeable estate and a probate, be sure your bill gets included. The administrator or executor will probably have the funds to pay you off.

If there are few assets and the relatives are divvying them up, give them the bill and explain that there is rent due. Usually they understand and will want to pay. Most people don't like the idea of the last memory of a loved one being contaminated with unpaid bills.

Of course, there's always the situation where there are no relatives and the state must dispose of the body and the personal property. Here an administrator will be appointed to oversee the disposal. Get your bill in right away and hope for the best.

CHAPTER 17

Returning the Security Deposit

The purpose of a deposit is to guarantee with money that the tenant will perform (or not perform) a certain act. With a deposit for a pet, for example, the landlord is hoping that by having the tenant put up a sum of money, it will guarantee that the tenant will see to it that the pet does not damage the property. With a cleaning deposit, the hope is that the deposit will ensure the tenant will keep the property clean, or at least clean it up thoroughly before leaving. Generally speaking, the bigger the deposit, the greater your security.

Real problems, however, can occur when it's time to return the deposit to the tenant. How much, if any, can the landlord keep? What kind of accounting must be done? When can the landlord use the deposits? Must the landlord pay interest on the deposit money while holding it? We'll cover these and other deposit concerns in this chapter.

LET TENANTS KNOW THEY'LL GET THE DEPOSIT BACK

When you collect a deposit, make it very clear to the tenant that you intend returning the money, providing that the conditions of the deposit are met. If the pet does no damage, you will promptly return *all* of the deposit. If the property is left as clean as it was found, and you have a method for determining this (such as walk-through inspection sheets), you will return all monies. If there is damage, you will subtract the cost of repairs and you have a reasonable method for determining costs.

Once the tenants become convinced that the deposit is not your advance Christmas present, they are usually willing to work with you. They'll take care of your property because they anticipate getting their money back.

WHERE DO I KEEP THE DEPOSIT?

Many landlords simply put rental deposits in their own personal account and spend them immediately as they would other income. There's apparently nothing illegal about this, although as a practical matter it can create some serious problems. For one, as soon as you put the money in your own account, you should probably declare it as income for tax purposes. For another, when the tenant moves out, you need to come up with the deposit money and what do you do if you've already spent it? Some landlords rob Peter to pay Paul. They quickly rerent the property and use the new tenant's deposit to pay the departing tenant—not a good practice.

SHOULD I USE A SEPARATE BANK ACCOUNT?

Most good property managers I know keep their rental deposits in a separate bank account. They have a special record book for keeping track

L A N D L O R D ' S   S T O R Y

I have seen some rather amazing real estate transactions take place on the basis of cleaning/security deposits. In one instance, the owner of an overpriced 105-unit apartment building in a very bad market gave her interest in the building away to a buyer, providing she could keep the cleaning deposits. Because the average rent of the building was $500 a month and she was holding around 100 deposits equal to one-and-a-half months' rent, she came away with $75,000. Of course, the new owners had to pay the tenants who eventually wanted their deposits back.

In another instance, a small group of investors took over an empty 500-unit apartment building, borrowing money for the down payment. They then quickly rented it up and used the security deposits they acquired, nearly $500,000, to pay back the down payment loan. In essence, the deposits helped finance the purchase!

This is not to say you should practice such creative financing. But it does point out the gray area into which deposits fall.

of the deposits and when tenants move out, they have the money available to either pay for repairs or to pay back the tenants. D money kept in this fashion may not be considered taxable income—t to your tax adviser.

There are two hidden problems here that new landlords don't usually appreciate. The first is mundane—namely, how do you create the separate bank account? The answer is that you can simply open an account in your name and then refer to it as the "John Smith Rental Deposit Account." Most banks won't bat an eye at setting it up that way and checks can be easily deposited to your "deposit account." Another more complex method is to set up a "trust account." This is more complex because you must keep very accurate records including who you're holding the money in trust for. Most real estate agents have these, although some banks may balk at setting them up for individuals.

The trust account gets into some difficulty with regard to the second hidden problem with deposits, namely, interest. If you accept a thousand dollar deposit and then stick it into a noninterest-bearing account, most people would say you're a fool. On the other hand, if you stick it into an interest-bearing account, who gets the interest? You, or the tenant whose money you're holding? In many states you can claim the interest for yourself, unless you stick the money in an account whose contents are "in trust" for someone else.

Legislation in some states now requires that landlords pay tenants at least a minimal amount of interest on deposit money. These rules often say something such as that landlords must pay the tenant 5 percent per annum on their money. Today, however, most savings accounts are paying less than 3 percent! Low interest rates have thrown the whole issue up into the air.

WHEN TO PAY BACK THE DEPOSIT

Most states have passed regulations determining how long a landlord can hang onto a deposit after a tenant moves out. For example, the landlord must pay back the deposit in full or give a complete accounting of how the money was spent within 21 days after a tenant moves out. The time limit varies, so be sure to check in your area.

Most tenants, understandably, do not want to wait 21 or more days. They may need the money as a deposit on the next place into which they

oom house which she rented to a minister. The man did not
ut he had excellent credit and his past history of renting was
raise the first month's rent and a cleaning deposit almost as
large and .... nth-to-month tenancy.

After about seven months, the minister called to say things just hadn't worked out with his new church. He was giving three weeks' notice (almost a month) and would be out on the 1st. He would leave the place clean and wanted and expected his cleaning deposit returned on the day he moved out. Sally explained it would be mailed to him within 14 days. He replied, "We'll see."

On the appointed day, Sally was at the property to receive the key. She had decided to forget the fact that she had received only three weeks' notice instead of a full month and went through the property with the minister conducting the "move-out, walk-through inspection" (described in Chapter 18). The property was generally clean, although there were a few things that needed attention and either the minister said he would fix them immediately or Sally said she would get it done. They agreed to her keeping $35 out of a $1,000 deposit. He then insisted on getting the remaining $965 at once. Sally balked, saying that she would send the money to him within 14 days, provided no other damage appeared. He said he would pay for any damage, but she would have to report it to him and then he would send her a check. He wanted his cleaning deposit now. She politely refused.

At that point he took her outside to the large mobile home he had parked in the driveway, filled with his belongings. He informed Sally that, God willing, the mobile home with him and his family living in it would move on the day she paid him his cleaning deposit and not a moment sooner.

Sally considered. He couldn't live in a mobile home in her driveway and they both knew it. But to get him to move she might have to call the police and even go to court. That would take time and suing a minister was no slam dunk. In the meantime, it would be hard to rerent the property with the minister and his family living in the driveway.

On the other hand, maybe he was bluffing. After all, he undoubtedly had his own business to attend to. She tried to compromise, saying she would give him half the deposit back now and half after two weeks. He was adamant. He wanted it all.

Sally could have argued more, but just didn't want the hassle. Sally finally gave in and gave him a check. He waved goodbye as he drove off.

As it turned out, the minister had inadvertently flushed a metal box down the drain and a plugged up sewer line turned up a few days later. The line had to be dug up at a cost of several hundred dollars.

When Sally contacted the minister about payment, he said he didn't remember flushing anything unusual down the drain. She pointed out that it could only have come from him, since he was the tenant in possession. They went round and round and eventually he sent her 50 bucks, far short of her costs.

The moral here is that it doesn't matter who your tenant is. Don't give the deposit back any sooner than the legal limit. You never know what will turn up. And it's far harder to collect your costs from a moved-out tenant than it is to write yourself a check from that tenant's deposit in your account.

are moving. And they are probably afraid that any delay at all means that you may not return all or most of the money to them. As a consequence, there is a kind of tug-of-war that occurs over the deposit at the time the tenants move out, with some tenants resorting to rather clever tactics to get their deposit back quickly.

But, a new landlord may ask, if the tenant leaves the property clean, why shouldn't I immediately return all of the deposit? Aha, I can hear experienced landlords saying, wait and see!

The reason has to do with hidden damage that may be found sometime after the tenant moves out. What's hidden damage? In one case, the tenant's children had flushed several toys down the drain and plugged it up. But this didn't show up until several days after they moved out, when a cleaning crew was at work in the house. In another case the tenant's pet had left the carpeting infested with fleas. The tenant had set off a flea bomb, killing all the mature fleas. It wasn't until two weeks later that flea eggs hatched, producing a house full of new biting insects, and the need to call a pest control company to get rid of them.

Wise landlords will hang onto that cleaning deposit as long as legally possible to ensure they have money to pay for any hidden damage found after the tenant moves out. As noted, however, tenants want that money right away and some will resort to creative methods to get it.

We've just seen how a tenant creatively handled the matter of getting the cleaning deposit back when he wanted it. There is another technique that tenants use much more frequently, however, and that's using the deposit as the last month's rent.

WHEN THE TENANT USES THE DEPOSIT AS THE LAST MONTH'S RENT

Today many landlords do not use a lease demanding first and last month's rent, but instead use a month-to-month rental agreement getting the first month's rent up front, plus a cleaning/security deposit equal to one month's rent. The idea here, of course, is that you don't have to automatically pay back the deposit and can instead use it to pay for damages. The last month's rent can only be applied to rent.

Many, dare I say most tenants, however, would be very pleased to consider that cleaning deposit as the last month's rent. In fact, they may take steps to ensure that it's the last month's rent.

L A N D L O R D ' S   S T O R Y

Hal rented a flat to college students for a nine-month period, collecting first month's rent plus a cleaning/security deposit equal to one month's rent.

The last month was June, the end of the school year, and when Hal went to receive the rent, he was told by the precocious students that they wouldn't pay the last month's rent. Instead, he was free to use the cleaning/security deposit for the rent. Of course, they said they would leave the flat spotless.

Hal did not like this one bit since it meant that when they moved, he would have no deposit left to cover any lack of cleaning or damage they might have done. He told them he would have them evicted. But, the students said that would take a month at the least and would be expensive. Besides, they would be out in 30 days so why bother? They said that any judge would probably feel the same way.

Hal said he would report them to a landlord's association and a credit report agency. They seemed surprised at his reaction and said he was being mean. After talking it over, however, they said that they were students anyhow, had no assets, and didn't care about their credit!

Hal reluctantly gave in. However, when they moved the place was a mess and it cost Hal nearly $500 out of pocket to get it in shape for the next tenants.

What could Hal have done to avoid this problem?

One answer is to not charge a month's rent as the cleaning/security deposit. If you charge exactly one month's rent, it's too convenient for the tenant to use it as the last month's payment. On the other hand, if you charge slightly less, it makes it harder for the tenant.

For example, let's say the rent is $1,000. Instead of charging $1,000 for the cleaning deposit, why not charge $965? The $35 isn't going to make much difference to you. Yet, the different amount makes a big psychological difference when it comes to trading the cleaning/security deposit for the rent.

Another thing to do is to stress big and bold in the rental agreement, **"This deposit may not be used for the last month's rent."** It gets the message across more clearly.

Yet another technique is to meet with the tenants as soon as possible before their planned move and carefully explain to them the consequences of taking such an action. One experienced property manager I know does this, carefully saying that if they try to use the cleaning deposit as the last month's rent, he would feel duty bound to report them to a credit reporting agency and this could affect their future ability to rent or buy another property and even their ability to get future credit including a credit card. When thus explained beforehand (instead of after the fact as Hal did in our example), most tenants are less inclined to take rash action.

Finally, it's important to make it perfectly clear to the tenants that you have their cleaning/security deposit safely in hand and that you fully intend and want to return it to them, provided they meet their obligations. If they see you are honest and well intentioned, they are going to be less inclined to try to use pressure against you.

SPECIAL PROBLEMS WITH PETS

Finally, there's the matter of the deposit for pets. My feeling, after having been burned many times, is that the deposit for pets should be very high indeed. As noted earlier, a single cat urinating on a carpet can destroy it, costing you thousands in replacement costs.

It's important to make clear to the tenant that your expectations are that the pet will use the great outdoors for its bathroom or that it will have a special litter box for use inside. Any damage to the carpet or the house will come out of the cleaning deposit. As you add hundreds of dollars to the pet deposit, you can almost see the deportment of the animal improve.

Note: It's probably a good idea to separate the pet deposit from the cleaning/security deposit. That emphasizes your special concern.

LANDLORD'S STORY

Hal had a nice house that he rented to a family with two dogs. He got a $1,000 pet deposit and felt quite secure.

Several months into the rental, the toilet backed up, flooding the apartment. The reason for the backup was a mystery. The tenant said the toilet had stuck and had kept on flushing, which was apparently true. The plumber said that he thought tree roots had gotten into the line, plugging it, and the additional water had then backed up. It was hard to blame the tenant for this. And in any event, Hal immediately had the carpets and padding taken out and sterilized—something which had to be done to avoid a health problem and potential landlord liability.

After the carpets were returned, the tenants complained the rugs smelled bad. Hal ignored them. At the end of their year, they moved out. When Hal inspected the property, he found that the dogs had urinated on the carpets, ruining them. He was furious and refused to return the deposit.

The tenants countered that the dogs had not urinated. Instead, Hal was smelling the remains of the sewer backup, about which they had complained. Eventually the tenants prevailed and Hal had to return their deposit.

Moral? Don't ignore tenants' complaints where a deposit is concerned. If Hal had taken action (such as having the carpets recleaned or replaced), the tenants would have no grounds for demanding their deposit back.

The Friendly Move-Out

You should never think of tenants as permanent. All tenants leave, sooner or later. Therefore, the goal of a good landlord (you!) is to make that eventual move-out as painless and as cost-free to you as possible. That means taking active steps to ensure that things go smoothly.

Good property managers know that the time to get started preparing for when the tenant moves out is on the day the tenant moves in. Many good managers on move-in day will hand the new tenants a printed sheet explaining just what's expected of them, including the procedure for moving out. It includes such things as giving notice and leaving the place clean. Don't think that all tenants automatically know how they are supposed to conduct themselves when they move out. Many are completely in the dark, unless you tell them. (See the appendix for a tenant move-out instruction sheet.)

A "moving instructions sheet" covers a number of areas that are important to the tenant and vital to you. Let's consider each in turn:

YOU MUST GIVE PROPER NOTICE

Assuming you're renting on a month-to-month basis, you're going to expect 30 days notice (or whatever you've agreed upon) before the tenant moves out. But just what constitutes notice? I once had tenants who included a note with a rent payment saying, "We will be moving soon."

A month later, they came by to drop off the key. When I asked what was up, they said they had given me written notice of their intention to move.

Inform tenants that you expect them to let you know the *exact date* when they intend to move out. For practical purposes, in most cases this will be in the form of a phone call. However, ideally they will send you a written note. And presumably their notice will be at least 30 days or whatever you've agreed upon before they moved in.

You should also indicate that you want the notice given *within 30 days of the next rent payment,* so that the tenant understands they are going to need to move on the 1st (presumably when the rent is due), not sometime in the middle of the following month. (Some states do allow notice to be given at any time—check in your area.)

A good idea is to include a tear-off at the bottom of the move-in sheet that they can send back to you which specifies just when they will move out.

Hint: If the tenant must move sometime other than on the rental date, you can, of course, agree to this. However, I would insist on the rent being paid until the 1st. If it's tenants who have given you trouble, of course, you may be happy to see them go and may be willing to compromise by splitting the difference.

WHAT MOVING OUT REALLY MEANS

It means that they will have *all* of their possessions out of the house and the garage and off the premises. Everything will be gone. There won't be clothes left hanging in a closet, boxes in the bedroom, or cooking utensils in the kitchen. Everything out means just that. Emphasize that you can't consider them out until they are fully out and have turned possession of everything in the rental back to you. (Anything they leave after that is presumably garbage which you will dispose of, billing them for cleaning and disposal costs.) Letting them know that you will require them to pay rent until everything is out helps assure compliance.

HOW AND WHEN THE DEPOSITS WILL BE RETURNED

Having a procedure and letting the tenants know what it is up front avoids confusion and unhappiness at the end. Let the tenants know you expect the property to be left in the same condition it was found, excepting normal wear and tear, and explain exactly what you mean.

Let them know that you will deduct from their deposits your costs for repairing damage that they do. If you have a pet deposit, indicate that you'll deduct from this any damage the pet may do. Indicate that any repair work will be done at the current market rate by professionals in the field, not by you. If you do repair work yourself, many tenants will assume your time is free and will not expect to be charged for it. Indeed, it may be illegal in your state or area for you to charge for *your time* spent on repair work on your own property.

Also let them know that they will receive the money back within 21 days, or as specified by the laws in your state, along with a complete accounting. This is a good place to put a notice in big type that the cleaning/security deposit may *not* be used as the last month's rent.

WHEN THE KEYS ARE TO BE RETURNED

At some point the tenants return possession of the property to you. This is normally done after they have removed all of their personal property and is evidenced by their returning the keys to you.

Be sure you let them know that you want *all* the keys returned. Even though you change the locks, you don't want someone out there who even thinks he or she can still get back in.

THEY MUST DISCONNECT UTILITIES AND PHONE

Normally the landlord has the utilities turned on for "clean-up and showing" on the same date as the tenant moves out. Point out that if they move later than the appointed date, they'll also be charged a prorated cost for utilities they use.

WHEN THEY NOTIFY YOU THAT THEY'RE GOING TO MOVE

As soon as you get wind of the fact that your tenants are going to move, it's a good idea to send them another one of the sheets noted above. They may have lost the original and this acts as a good reminder.

LETTER OF RECOMMENDATION

If I have a good tenant who always pays on time and didn't cause a problem, I usually call and ask them if they would like a letter of recommendation for their next landlord. Most tenants are astounded at this offer and, of course, happily accept.

I have no problem recommending a good tenant to someone else. Further, giving them this letter often puts the tenant in such a friendly state of mind that they do an extra good job of cleaning up the property, just to live up to what I've said about them! (Check the appendix for a typical recommendation letter.)

Note that if tenants move out in order to purchase a property, their mortgage lender will almost certainly request a formal letter from you asking for specifics on the tenant. Giving a copy to the tenant showing how you recommended them does the same thing as the separate letter noted above.

CONFIRM MOVING DATES

A good landlord quickly learns not to leave anything to guesswork or chance. The tenants have said they would be out by August 1st. Great, it's the middle of July, so call them to confirm the date. Also confirm that they received the "move-out instructions" sheet. And reconfirm that they understand what's required to get the cleaning/security deposit back.

It shouldn't be necessary for you to go this extra step, but if you don't, there will come a time when you think they're moving out on one day and they'll be moving out on another. Don't think: Confirm!

When it gets close to the actual move-out date, call again. Arrange for a time for them to meet you in the rental to go through the "move-out walk-through" (see the appendix for an example move-out sheet). Also, emphasize that at that time, they will need to have all of their personal property out of the house and will need to return the keys.

MEET WITH THE TENANTS AT MOVE-OUT TIME

When you meet with the tenants on the appointed day for their departure, you should immediately check to see that they are completely out

L A N D L O R D ' S   S T O R Y

Hal had a rental on the other side of town. It was a good property that rented easily, but he had to take the busy cross-town expressway to get to it and that was inconvenient, so he went out there as rarely as possible.

One day his tenants called to let him know they'd be moving the next month and he made a mental note of it. They called again a week before they were to move and let him know it would be on a Sunday and they'd be out by noon. He could come by at that time and check out the property and get the keys back. Hal again made a mental note of it, which he promptly forgot.

It was a week-and-a-half later on a Wednesday that Hal thought about the rental, mainly because he hadn't received the rent. He then remembered the tenants said they were moving on the previous Sunday. He called them, but the phone was disconnected, so he drove out there, much to his irritation, on the busy cross-town freeway.

He found the front door open and the tenants gone. The flooring and carpeting was a mess because neighborhood kids had apparently wandered in with muddy shoes and tracked it up. Other than that, however, it was clean and in good shape. The keys were on the counter along with a note saying the tenants had cleaned the apartment and waited for him that Sunday until 2 PM. They had called, but had been unable to get through. When they had to leave, they locked the doors, left the keys on the counter, and a forwarding address for their deposit to be returned.

Hal promptly had the apartment cleaned and deducted the cost along with three days' rent until he picked up the keys. The tenants protested. They said they had made every effort to contact Hal and return the keys on the day they left. They said they had left the apartment spotless and the doors locked and had no idea how the neighborhood kids had gotten in. And they produced a copy of their letter to Hal which they had left on the counter.

Hal wanted to stonewall them, but on advice from a property manager friend, decided to avoid a hassle when he was told he couldn't win. He returned all of their deposit. After all, the loss of three days and the extra cleaning were entirely due to his own lack of attention.

of the rental unit. Furniture, boxes, clothing, and so on left anywhere indicates that they are not out. You should point this out to them and indicate that you can't proceed until they have *all* of their possessions removed. If necessary, tell them you'll come by later, although you can emphasize that this will be an inconvenience to you. If it takes them another day to get their possessions out, you can point out that you will have to deduct a day's rent from their deposit.

Assuming that they are completely out, you should ask them for the keys to the unit, making sure they return all sets. Once they have moved their personal property out and given you the keys, they have returned possession to you.

Now, it's time to go over the "walk-through inspection sheet" with them (see the appendix). (You can do this before you receive the keys, of course, but I like to get the keys first indicating that they are finished with the cleaning.)

THE MOVE-OUT WALK-THROUGH INSPECTION

This sheet is the same one that you used for these tenants when they moved in. Presumably you've kept it safely stored awaiting the day they move out.

The idea is that you bring it out, or a copy of it, and then you go over it, room by room, with the tenants. Along the way you discover any damage that's more than "normal wear and tear" and you and they account for it, indicating what damage will be deducted from their cleaning deposit.

When you're finished, you've agreed upon damages—if not exact amounts, everyone shakes hands, and you've successfully concluded the tenancy.

Not likely. That's the ideal scenario. In actual practice it's rarely that simple. Let's consider what's more likely to happen.

Tenants Don't Show Up for the Move-Out Walk-Through Inspection

It's to their advantage to show up, you point out. They can be on hand to dispute any damage that you feel may be charged against them. They point to the inspection record and note that the damage was right there before they moved in.

True. In most cases tenants will show up for the move-out walk-through inspection. But in some cases they won't. Maybe their schedule makes it impossible for them to be there. Maybe they left the place in such a mess that they're too embarrassed to show up. Or maybe they just can't handle the apparent confrontation involved in walking through with you.

In any event, it isn't necessary for the tenants to be there for the move-out walk-through inspection. Their not being there doesn't prevent you from conducting the inspection yourself, it only weakens their position should they dispute anything you say later on.

My own feeling is that if the tenants aren't there for the move-out walk-through inspection, I want to document anything I find. This can mean having a neutral third party, such as a neighbor, walk through with me and sign that what I say I found is indeed the way it was. Or it could also include taking photos or videos of damage. (Remember, in an earlier chapter I noted the problems with taking these beforehand because it was difficult to photograph clean areas because you wouldn't know where the damage would occur? Now, there's no problem. You can zero right in on the damage.)

Tenants Show Up and Walk Through with You, But Deny They Did Any of the Damage

This is what can happen: You walk into a bedroom and there are crayon marks all over the walls. You point this out to the tenant and say that this can't be washed off without ruining the paint. Instead, the walls will have to be thoroughly washed, then painted twice, once with a sealer to keep any remaining crayon marks from bleeding through, and a second time for the actual painting.

The tenants look aghast and say that their kids couldn't possibly have done the damage. Maybe a little bit of it, but the walls were definitely marked beforehand. Now you both turn to the sheet on this bedroom that the tenants initialed when they first moved in and look to see what's written there.

You hope it will say, "All walls clean and freshly painted—no marks or scratches of any kind." You point to this and what can the tenant argue about?

Instead, however, it says, "Walls generally clean with a few marks and scratches."

"Aha!" The tenants say, "See, we told you. It was marked up before we moved in."

Once again this points out the importance of being extremely careful and precise when you fill out these walk-through sheets. Remember my telling you to list each mark by size, shape, and location?

You are going to be hard-pressed to keep any of the tenants' cleaning/security deposit if your own sheets note there were marks and scratches on the walls before they moved in. On the other hand, you're going to be in an excellent position to use the deposit to clean up the damage if your sheets indicate no marks or scratches were there beforehand.

Hint: Always paint and clean your rental thoroughly before the tenants move in. That way you'll be able to write down a clean bill-of-paint on the move-in walk-through inspection sheet, which will provide you with the evidence you need to collect for damages when you conduct the move-out walk-through inspection.

Tenants Agree They Did the Damage, But Now Want to Correct It Themselves

If you did your move-in walk-through sheet correctly, there really won't be much disputing over who did the damage to your rental. There will be the tenants' own signature and initials on a written document saying there were no marks, scratches, and so on when they moved in. And now, here's the damage. Yes, they can still always deny it, but anyone based in reality is going to see that theirs is a losing cause.

So now the tenant may say something such as, "Yes, I didn't realize how marked up those walls really were. I'm surprised, but I'd like the opportunity to correct it myself."

Letting the tenant who did the damage correct it after they move out is like giving an award to the person who helps put out the fire in your barn after they set it. This is a trap that is very difficult to avoid. The tenants have already moved out and, presumably, given you the keys. Now, the tenants want the opportunity to go back and clean up or fix damage that you both agree they did.

You may argue that they should have corrected the damage before they moved. However, if the tenant now gets angry and eventually drags you into small claims court they can argue they offered to fix the damage, once it was revealed to them, but you didn't give them the opportunity to do so. Not giving them the opportunity to correct a problem, once it's revealed, could mean you'd lose.

You're in a sort of lose-lose situation. If you don't give them the opportunity to fix up/clean up, it could come back to haunt you. But, if you do give them the opportunity, it could be even worse.

When the Tenant "Corrects" the Problem

In our example, there were crayon marks on the walls. The problem here is that the grease in crayons bleeds through most paints. The easiest way to handle this is as noted earlier: wash, seal, and repaint.

However, a tenant who's already vacated the premises isn't likely to want to take the time to go through the various steps, which can take a couple of days. When this situation once happened to me and I let the tenant attempt the cleanup, she used a heavy industrial cleaner on the walls, rubbing hard to remove the crayon marks. Not the easiest way to go, but very thorough. Too thorough.

She did remove the marks, but she also removed the paint and some of the plaster where she had rubbed. Now instead of crayon marks, there were paintless areas and gouges in the plaster that stood out distinctly from the other areas of the wall. It would require not only painting, but replastering and retexturing to correct. The price was going up.

The tenant, however, proudly pointed to the area upon reinspection and dared me to find any crayon marks on the wall!

In a situation where a tenant wants time to correct the problem, I try to point out the obvious. In attempting to correct it, it may be made worse. Further, I need to get in quickly to clean up so that it can be shown and rerented. If the tenant wants time to do further cleanup, then I'll just have to assume that they have possession during that time and deduct daily rent while they're cleaning.

When I point out the problems involved and the timing concerns, frequently the tenants back off of their desire to do it themselves. I've found that most tenants who do damage aren't really that anxious to spend a lot of physical effort correcting the problem.

DISPUTES OVER PRICE

Matters may now evolve to a question of how much it will it cost to have the repairs done. As I mentioned, I no longer do the work myself. Now, we're talking about having someone come in, wash the wall, seal it, and then repaint. How much for that?

I have a person who can do that for around $50 per wall, plus the cost of the materials. I give that figure to the tenants, who may acquiesce, figuring it's worth it just to avoid any hassle.

This, however, brings up a point that's in dispute among property managers. Some managers prepare a pricing chart, an actual list of prices for various services they may perform on a rental. There's a price for cleaning a clogged drain and repainting a wall with crayon marks on it. There's a price for fixing a broken window and cleaning a stain out of the carpet. In short, there's a price listed for almost everything.

When there's a dispute such as noted above, the landlord brings out the list, points to the price for repainting a wall with crayon marks, and says, "That's $65, including materials." There it is in black and white. It's so clear-cut and easy. Many managers will even make their pricing list available to tenants when they first move in and again when they give notice they are moving out so that there won't be any confusion over costs.

A list is indeed neat and clean and I have no argument with those who use it. But, I don't like it myself for two reasons. First, prices change and change often. That means I would have to be constantly updating my list. I'm simply not organized enough to be doing that all the time for a whole variety of costs. Besides, I find that much of the work is done by a handyperson, they change frequently, and each tends to charge differently.

Secondly, lists tend to be overly restricting. By that I mean that the problem may not fit the list's description or the price given. For example, the drain's clogged. How much does your list charge for that?

It all depends, of course, on what the problem is. It could be only $55 to have the rooter man come out and run a snake through the lines. Or it could be $700 to dig up a blockage caused by a having a steel rod flushed down the line until it wedged at an elbow joint. This actually happened to me when I rented to a mechanic who worked in a body and fender shop, and his child somehow got one of his tools into the drain system.

After awhile, you get a pretty good idea of what things will cost and you can give an *estimate* to the tenant right on the spot. If, on the other hand, the tenants don't like your price or you're not sure of the cost, you can say, "I'll have someone come in to look at it immediately and she'll tell me the cost. I'll get back to you on that."

Admittedly, this isn't the best of all possible solutions because it takes time. But it does have the advantage of ending up with an accurate price.

And quite frankly, by the next day, the tenant is even less inclined to dispute the pricing.

THE VALUE OF HAVING THE TENANT WALK THROUGH WITH YOU

As difficult as it can be at times, having the tenant go through the move-out walk-through inspection with you has one enormous benefit. You usually end up with agreement at the end.

The tenant being there forces you to be fair in your estimates (not that you wouldn't be anyhow, of course). Your being there forces the tenant to see things from your perspective and to acknowledge that some damage may have actually been done.

In short, the tenant is more likely to accept deductions from the cleaning/security deposit after the walk-through. And, in my opinion, the tenant is far less likely to feel angered and get into a dispute with you that ends up in court. In other words, even though at times it can be hard on the blood pressure, walking through with the tenant can end up being the most amicable way of ending a tenancy, especially one in which there's going to be deductions from the tenant's deposit.

WHEN TO RETURN THE DEPOSIT

As noted earlier, give the deposit money back promptly in accordance with the laws of your state. But hang onto it long enough to uncover any hidden damage which may have occurred.

I have, on occasion, given back a portion (as much as half) of the deposit right on the spot at the time the tenant moved out if, after going through the move-out walk-through inspection, nothing obvious appeared. Yes, I realize this is not good property management practice because a large hidden cost could crop up later. But I do sympathize with tenants who worry about somebody else holding their money and who need it right away to move into another property.

You, of course, must make your own decisions.

Your Insurance Requirements

For a moment, let's ask what is the worst that's likely to happen to you as a landlord? Is it having the rental burn down? Is it not being able to find tenants to rent the premises? Is it having a tenant leave the property a mess?

LIABILITY INSURANCE

Actually, although the chances of it happening are very slim, the worst that could happen to you probably is to have a tenant sue you for injury on your property . . . and you not be fully covered by insurance. Your property might be worth $150,000, but you could be liable for hundreds of thousands of dollars or more in damages. This applies whether you own the property or are managing it for someone else. (You can be assured that in any suit both the owner and the managing landlord—if they are different—will be named.) Therefore, it behooves you to carry full liability insurance. It covers you for many things related to a property and for which you can be sued.

Thus, the question is not whether or not you should have liability insurance—you should. It's how much to carry.

Many property management firms say that you should carry between $300,000 and $500,000 in liability insurance. I think their reasoning stems from the fact that many insurance companies today limit the liability coverage you can get on a single-family rental property to those amounts.

However, umbrella policies are available from many companies which cover excess liability. They take over when your regular liability insurance ends and provide coverage above that amount. A few years ago I was involved with a condominium rental project that had more than 100 units and we regularly carried a minimum of $15 million in liability insurance.

Although liability premiums are constantly rising, the point to remember is that after you pay your basic premium for the $300,000 or $500,000 or whatever, the umbrella excess coverage is actually quite cheap. I think the reasoning by the insurance companies is that their risk is greatest for the first $100,000 and decreases dramatically after that. Maybe so, but I suggest you let them worry about statistical risk. To sleep well at night, I prefer an umbrella over me reaching in the millions.

FIRE INSURANCE

If you have a mortgage on your property, you almost certainly are required to carry, at minimum, basic fire insurance. This simply means that if the building burns down, your *lender* gets paid. However, you want to carry enough fire insurance so that *you* have your interest in the building protected as well. In other words, you want your equity saved.

In the old days, insurance companies used to only offer a form of insurance that would pay a cash settlement amount. For example, you would insure your property for $100,000 and that's what you would get if the building burnt down. If you owed $80,000, the lender would get that money and you'd get the remainder, or $20,000.

Today, however, most insurance polices involve some sort of replacement cost. In other words, if your building burns down, the insurance company will rebuild the property so that you are back where you started. (Except, of course, that you end up with a brand new building instead of an older one.) In some cases they will also make the mortgage payments during the rebuild period.

If all this sounds terrific, be aware that there are a lot of pitfalls along the way that you need to be wary of.

Replacement Cost Insurance

When you buy your insurance, you must specifically ask for replacement cost insurance. If your policy doesn't specifically say you have it, you may not. Check with your insurance agent.

Be aware that there are two types of replacement cost insurance—standard and guaranteed. Under the standard form, your property is depreciated and you only get the depreciated value, which may not be enough to replace it. Under the guaranteed form, the insurance company replaces your property regardless of the cost. Guaranteed replacement cost has only recently become available from many insurance companies on rental properties. Also, some guaranteed insurance has limits, say 125 percent of the insured amount. Be aware of exactly what type of coverage you are buying.

Amount of Insurance Coverage

As a condition of your mortgage, virtually all lenders require that you carry a *minimum* amount of fire insurance. Typically, they will want you to carry enough to cover the mortgage amount. That, however, may actually be too much coverage!

Today, in parts of the country where real estate values are high, a significant portion of the cost of a piece of property is the land value. In some cases the land values may be 50 percent or more of the total property value. The thing about land, however, is that it doesn't burn. So why insure it? (Because the lender demands it.)

Perhaps an example will help. You have property with a total worth of $300,000; the land is worth $150,000 of that amount. When you purchase it, you get an 80 percent mortgage or $240,000. Naturally enough, the lender wants you to carry $240,000 worth of fire insurance. That's unrealistic, however, because your building's value is only $150,000. Rest assured the premium on that extra $90,000 is going to cost you a pretty penny. Unfortunately, while you can argue, most lenders prefer to be safe than sorry and will insist on the additional coverage, which they usually can enforce as part of the loan agreement you sign.

EXTENDED OR HOMEOWNER'S INSURANCE

In the past, extended or homeowner's coverage was not always available to rental property owners. Today, however, this coverage is available for single family to four-unit buildings from some insurers and the cost is often only a small amount over and above the standard policy. This covers you for a large number of risks in addition to fire, including damage caused by storms, aircraft crash, smoke, burst pipes (not the pipes, but the damage caused by the water), vandalism, falling trees, landslides, and much more. If it is available, you definitely should carry this extra coverage.

EARTHQUAKE/FLOOD/STORM ENDORSEMENTS OR POLICIES

In California you want earthquake insurance. In parts of the Midwest you want flood insurance. In Florida and along the Gulf Coast you might need hurricane insurance.

Unfortunately, if you are in a high risk area, chances are that this kind of insurance is not available through the normal channels. Most insurance companies simply won't cover the risk at any cost. However, there may be pooled risk insurance available or the federal or state government may offer it (such as the Federal Flood Program), often at a reasonable cost. Check with a good insurance agent.

Caution: Natural calamity insurance—such as earthquake, flood, and storm insurance—often has strict limitations. It may have a very high deductible and the total coverage may be limited. Further, a major storm or flood could wipe out an insurance pool's reserves, meaning that you might only get partial payment. It's something to consider.

OTHER COVERAGE TO CHECK OUT

In addition to the coverages mentioned above, you may want to ask your agent about adding the following coverages or you may want to check with a different insurer who does offer them.

Vandalism

Usually covered under an extended fire insurance coverage, this is becoming increasingly important. Today one vandal with one can of spray paint can do thousands of dollars of damage to your property in a few minutes. Broken windows, break-ins, and other forms of vandalism are also increasing. You want insurance to cover you against these.

Inflation Guard

This coverage automatically ups the value of your insurance annually, usually based on some index such as the Consumer Price Index. The idea here is that the same property costs more to replace each year. With this coverage, you shouldn't unexpectedly find that you are not fully insured due to inflation.

Demolition/Code Upgrade

When you have a loss, your property will often only be partially destroyed (although it may be a total economic loss). That means that someone has to come in and bulldoze the wreck. Unless you have a special demolition endorsement, this may not be covered by your policy.

Similarly, if you have an older property, the building code in your area may have been upgraded since your rental was built. It may cost more to replace it today simply because the newer building codes are stricter. This type of endorsement pays the additional cost of reconstruction due to changes in building codes.

Loss of Rents

You'll want to check to be sure this coverage is in your policy. It guarantees that while your property is uninhabitable because of fire or other calamity, you get paid your rents as if it were fully occupied. This allows you to continue making your mortgage and other payments.

Glass Breakage, Equipment, Waterbed, Mortgage, and More

Don't automatically assume that everything is covered in your policy. Many areas may require special endorsements or even separate policies. Of course, there are endorsements available for almost any type of risk. The best bet is to find a good insurance agent to go over your property concerns with you. You may find you need much more coverage . . . or much less!

Also, study your deductible and your maximum amount covered. These limits, too, can be changed by a special endorsement.

TENANT'S INSURANCE

Many new landlords are surprised to discover that their extended coverage policy does not cover the personal property of tenants. If there's a broken pipe, for example, and some of the tenants' furniture is destroyed, your policy may not cover it. This, however, would only encourage the tenants to sue you for damages because of the broken pipe.

In the past it was usually necessary for a tenant to show negligence on the landlord's part in order to win a lawsuit involving the rental. Increasingly, however, it's becoming the case that the tenants only have to show that there's a defect in the property. This could have important consequences for you if the tenants or their possessions are damaged.

There is a way for tenants to cover their belongings, however, and that's tenant's insurance. It's widely available and it's roughly the sort of insurance that you get with a homeowner's policy. Extended fire policies are available that usually protect tenants from a wide variety of risks, from fire to having their dog bite someone. But generally speaking, tenants must insure their own belongings.

When they move in, always tell tenants that their belongings are not covered under your insurance policy. Encourage them to get their own tenant's policy.

WORKER'S COMPENSATION

Worker's compensation pays a worker when he or she is injured on the job. But, you may say, you aren't hiring anyone, so why do you need worker's comp?

The answer is that you may hire an independent contractor to do anything from mow your lawn to fix your roof. Presumably, that independent contractor carries worker's compensation. But, if he doesn't and if someone is injured on the job while working for you, you can almost be certain that the injured person will come to you for compensation. It's at that point your worker's comp should cut in.

In some states, worker's comp is required to be included on all broad coverage insurance. In others, it is not. Be sure to check your policy and with your agent to see what kind of coverage you have. If you don't have worker's comp, I strongly urge you to get it. The premium is typically not very high for a landlord (or property owner) when added to an extended policy and it usually is well worth the expense.

FINDING THE RIGHT INSURANCE COMPANY

Here are some points to watch for when choosing your insurance company:

Ratings

Insurance companies are rated by several firms, probably the most well known being Best. Go for an insurance company with a Best rating of at least A and preferably A+.

Agents

Check out the agents. Some are independents and can give you quotes from a variety of companies. Others write only for one company. Get several quotes and compare the cost against what you get. And be sure that you're covered! Demand proof of coverage when you pay your premium. Otherwise if the agent delays sending in your policy and catastrophe strikes, you might not have coverage.

Deductibles

Consider this carefully. Many companies will offer significantly reduced premiums for higher deductibles. For example, you might cut your policy cost in half if you accept a $1,000 deductible as opposed to a $100 deductible.

But, you may argue, think of the $900 you could lose in the event of a claim!

That's exactly what I am thinking about. By accepting a higher deductible, you are, in effect, self-insuring your property. This may be a good idea. Consider if you have a claim for $800. You have a $100 deductible so the insurance company pays you $700. But the next time your premium comes along, it may go up. Or you may find that your insurer really doesn't want your business any more.

On the other hand, if you have a $1,000 deductible and you pay the $700 claim yourself, you don't turn it in to your insurance company. Now you have the benefits of a lower premium, plus your insurer loves you because you don't have any claims.

The point is that you're going to end up paying either way. With a higher deductible and self-insurance for small claims, you may save money in the long run and end up with a better insurer and a better policy.

LOOK FOR PREMIUM SAVERS

Most insurance companies offer reduced premiums for certain types of equipment. For example, if you have a smoke detector in the property (often a mandatory requirement of your building and safety code), your premium may be reduced. Similarly there may be reductions for fire extinguishers kept on the property and for sprinkler or security alarm systems. Check with your insurance company to see how you can save.

BE CAREFUL WITH CLAIMS

I have a cynical friend who says that the entire purpose of many insurance companies is to collect premiums and deny claims. Don't expect your insurance company to instantly take your word for everything and pay you what you want. You need to document any claims, particularly those that involve injury. (Of course, be sure that the injured party immediately receives appropriate medical care.)

Get statements from witnesses, if appropriate. Keep the invoices for all work that you have done. Pay by check and when you get your cancelled check back from the bank, hang onto it as proof that you paid for work done. (Yes, there are still banks today that will send back cancelled checks, if you demand it!) Keep a diary, if possible, recounting all incidents. And report claims promptly to your insurer.

Raising the Rent

From a landlord's perspective, there is only one direction rents should go: upward. Unfortunately, the rental market in any given area is always changing and not always for the better. Some years it's a landlord's market, with more tenants chasing fewer rentals. Other years it's a tenant's market, with more landlords chasing fewer tenants. The truth of the matter is that you can only charge what the market will bear. Charge too high a rental rate and you'll have a vacancy.

As a result, you must watch the market carefully. Sometimes to keep a good tenant, you may actually want to lower your rates. Do it. You will astonish the tenant and avoid the hassle of clean-up and the difficulty of rerenting when there are too many vacancies around.

You can't always get the rents you want, but you can always get what the market will bear.

HOW TO DETERMINE THE MARKET RATE

Whether you're renting for the first time or thinking about raising rents, you should always first check out the market. How do you do this?

There are a variety of ways, but the simplest is to look in the local paper where rentals are advertised. Let's say yours is a single family home: three bedrooms, two baths, and a fireplace. Now check out the paper for homes for three bed/two bath homes with a fireplace *in the same area as*

L A N D L O R D ' S   S T O R Y

A few years ago, Hal bought an eight-unit rental property in Phoenix, Arizona. He had been told that Phoenix was growing at a phenomenal rate, something like 5 percent a year. Yet, residential property was amazingly cheap. His plan was simple—buy property, hold it a few years while renting it out, then sell at a profit.

What he didn't realize was that at the time, housing was increasing at well over 5 percent a year. There were far more homes being built than buyers, or tenants, in the area. In other words, it was a terrible market.

Almost from the moment he bought the property, things began to turn downward. The eight-unit apartment building he bought had been fully rented. But after taking it over, he realized that most of the tenants were nonpaying. The former owner had "doctored" the books.

Hal kicked out six nonpaying tenants and then tried to rerent the units. Only he quickly found that in the highly competitive market, other landlords were offering one or even two months' rent free. Some were offering free TVs or microwaves to anyone who would move in. Some were offering to rent without cleaning or security deposits.

Hal, on the other hand, figured out how much income he would need to cover his expenses, divided by eight, and asked that much for each unit. For the two currently occupied units, that meant a rent increase. By the end of the month, the two remaining tenants moved out.

Hal now had a completely empty eight-unit apartment building that stayed empty for five months. At that time, Hal bailed out of the market, selling the building to an investor who just took over for the mortgage payments. Hal lost his equity. The new investor cut the rental rate, filled up the building, hung onto it for four years, and eventually sold at a hefty profit.

your rental. It's usually best to do this with the Sunday paper, because usually more rentals are shown there.

Within just a few minutes you can get a good idea of what properties about the same size, location, and features as yours are renting for. If another property has a pool, deduct a bit from what you can get. If yours has a bigger yard or an extra family room, add a bit. Your figures won't be 100 percent accurate, but they probably will be close.

Now, take an afternoon and go to see a half dozen similar rentals in your property's area. Within a very short time, you should be able to get a highly accurate sense of what the market is for your rental. Be sure to ask landlords how long they've had their property on the market and if there are any reductions, for example, for signing a year's lease.

This should give you a good place to start in determining for how much you can rent your property.

Another method is to call several local real estate agents whose offices specialize in the management of rentals. Describe your property. You can say you're considering using a property management firm, which you may very well be doing. Usually they will be happy to send someone over to tell you what they think you can get in rent. Check with three or four firms and you'll have an extremely accurate estimation of your optimum rental rate. These experts also can quickly let you know if there are any move-in bonuses that are common in your area such as gifts, free rent, or something else.

Yet another method is to join the local rental property owners association, if there is one in your area. These organizations can give you lists of rental rates and can also provide leases and other forms most suited to your area.

Thus, with a day or two of work, you should be able to quickly and easily determine the market rental rate for your unit.

DON'T BE STUBBORN WHEN IT COMES TO THE MARKET

Your property will rent for whatever amount the market will bear and that has no relation to what your expenses are. One of the greatest mistakes a landlord can make is to try to fight the market. You want $750 a month, but the market will only bear $700. So you stubbornly hold out for your money. Eventually, four months later, you find a tenant who's willing to pay your rate and you exult at your victory. But have you won or lost?

Consider: it took you four months to find this tenant. That's $2,800 in lost rent that you presumably would have received by renting immediately at the market rate of $700 a month. But, of course, you're now getting $50 a month more. The trouble is, it's going to take you 56 months— more than four years—to recoup the lost four months of rent. Renting immediately for $700, you might have been able to raise the rents $50 a month after one year.

Remember, it's a lot worse to have a property vacant than to have it rented full time at a lower rate than you want. Your goal is to get as close to 100 percent occupancy as possible. If you drop below 90 percent occupancy, then you're probably charging too high a rental rate.

WHEN TO RAISE RENTS

Some landlords raise the rents every year a tenant stays in the property. It's kind of like a penalty for renting from them. The longer the tenant stays there, the more the tenant has to pay. Of course, with these landlords, tenants rarely stay long.

In my opinion, there are three conditions that all must be in effect before you raise the rents:

1. *You must have more money from the rental.* If you're in a negative cash flow situation, you probably won't survive long holding onto the property. Either you won't have the funds to continue or your will to stick it out will be worn down. Any rental property worth its salt should at least break even. (That's after all considerations including extra income from washing machines, vending machines, extra car space, and so on, as well as all write-offs including depreciation.) You need to raise the rents.

2. *The market will bear an increase.* You've done your homework and found out what other rentals are charging. You are charging less. You probably will be able to sustain a rental increase.

3. *The tenants feel you are justified in raising rates.* Your goal is not to have the tenants move out. Rather, your goal is to keep the same tenants, only get a higher rental rate. To accomplish this, the tenants must feel that you are justified in raising rates. The tenants will feel this way if you handle the increase in a civilized manner (with respect for the tenants' feelings), present a logical case including market analysis of other rental rates, and assure them that there won't be another increase very soon. When they check it out and discover that you're correct, they'll probably stay.

THE COST-OF-MOVING FACTOR

You should be aware that tenants almost always consider the cost of moving. If you are charging the current market rate, you can often successfully raise the rents a bit more, depending on what it costs for the tenants to move someplace else. For example, let's say the typical costs of moving are $1,000. You might successfully raise the rent $50 a month on a year's lease, even though that's $50 higher than market rate. Over a year it only comes to $600, less than the cost of moving someplace else.

Hint: Don't overlook the "inertia factor." Most people don't like to move. It's a hassle. The kids might have to change schools. As a result, your tenants may stay simply because it's easier than moving. Of course, increase the rents high enough and you'll drive any tenant out.

Should You Hire a Property Management Firm?

We've already talked at length about problem tenants and all the troubles they can cause you. Of course, there's always eviction, the ultimate solution.

However, sometimes you don't want to evict a problem tenant, particularly one who pays the rent or is in a unit that's particularly difficult to rerent. You may have a tenant you want to keep, but who just keeps giving you all sorts of headaches. If that's the case, then a property management firm may be just the answer for you.

In the case that follows the outside property management firm plays an important role—that of intermediary. The firm steps between you and the tenant and gives you some distance. Further, it is often better able to deal with the tenant because it can always say, "Well, you know the owner insists that we raise the rent. What can we do? We're just the managers." Just as a real estate agent acts as a kind of referee between buyer and seller, the property management firm can act as a kind of go-between between you and the tenant. It can tell the tenant something unpleasant for them to hear, such as that the rent's going up or that their dirty house is the cause of them having spiders. And if the tenants get mad, it's usually at the bearer of the bad news, the property management firm, not you, the owner.

When a tenant gets too frustrating to deal with, when a property gets too hard to handle, it may be time to call for outside help. In the long run it could not only make it easier for you to sleep at night, but it could also save you money.

L A N D L O R D ' S   S T O R Y

Sally had a single family house with a pool that she rented out to a lovely couple with two charming, small children. They seemed to be wonderful people, concerned with their environment, anxious about the condition of the house, eager to get their rent in on time.

But as soon as they moved in, they began complaining. The screen door didn't slide easily. There were ants in the house, then they found a big spider. The carpets weren't clean enough. The windows didn't lock properly. The pool cleaning person didn't come often enough.

Of course, Sally responded to all of the complaints quickly, but often they were trivial. For example, she called an exterminator for the ants. Then, she called him back for the spider. But he explained he wouldn't guarantee a spiderless house. The only way to keep them out was to get rid of all the cobwebs in the corners and elsewhere. Then she called a handyperson to work on the windows and the sliding screen door, but he couldn't find a problem.

The tenants did pay their rent on time and it was an older house in a not-so-wonderful neighborhood, so Sally didn't want to lose them. But their weekly (or more often) calls became extremely annoying. Further, because they talked to her so often, she began to feel they were becoming overly familiar and began expecting favors. Like the time a few months later when they called to tell her their rent would be a week late, but they were sure she would understand and that they could count on her friendship.

Finally, Sally began to realize that these tenants, though probably not doing it consciously, were getting under her skin and keeping her from being a good landlord. The final straw was when she planned on raising the rent and realized she just couldn't make herself tell them. She had become an ineffective landlord.

So Sally hired a professional property management firm. They charged her 10 percent of the rental income. But, they raised rents the first month by 10 percent and so quickly paid for their cost. More to the point, they fielded all the complaints effectively and for the first time in a long time, Sally could relax and not dread the phone ringing for fear it was her problem tenants.

WHEN THE PROPERTY IS TOO FAR AWAY

Another good reason to have a property management firm is when you own property too far from your home. Let's face it, for most of us it's a mistake to buy distant rentals. We can't always be there to rent them. We can't easily handle maintenance or repairs. We can't pop right over when the tenant has a crisis. We can't be there when the rent's late. In short, we can't be a good landlord at a distance.

But, for a fee, a property management firm can do all of these things for us. It can be your representative right on the spot.

WHEN THE PROPERTY IS TOO BIG

Finally, the property may simply be too big for you to manage personally. It's one thing if you only own a single family rental, or even an eight-unit apartment building. But what if you have 100 units or more? You could wear yourself ragged trying to keep up with the tenants. In this case, a property management firm may very well pay for itself.

A number of computer programs can handle the book work of property management for you. Look into *EZ-Units* by 3G Software, available from 2-Law (800-526-5588).

CHAPTER 22

Rentals and the IRS

Note: While it's beyond the scope of this book to get into detailed tax considerations of real estate, some insights into problems associated with property taxation might be useful. Please note that the following information is not comprehensive. You should check with your tax specialist for details.

Renting property is a taxing proposition in many ways, not the least of which is dealing with the federal government in terms of taxation. Basically, running a rental is like running a business. You have income—from rents, washing machines, etc., and you have expenses—mortgage payments, insurance, property taxes, and so on. The only way you can know if you have profits or losses is to subtract expenses from income. If you have a profit, you'll need to pay taxes on it. If you have a loss, you may be able to apply it elsewhere, or in some circumstances, write it off of your regular income (see the end of this chapter for more on this).

The Internal Revenue Service requires that you keep documentation for all income and expenses so that you can substantiate them, if called upon to do so. The last thing you want is for the government to challenge your expenses or income and for you to not be able to come up with written invoices and receipts to prove what you claim.

THE PAPER TRAIL

If you own a small number of rental units, you don't need a fancy system for keeping records. You can buy a filing box with separators in it and make divisions for each property and even headings under different properties. Within each property division, you can keep a separate folder for electrical repairs, plumbing repairs, pool maintenance, gardening, and so forth. For example, you'll have a division for the Rover Street house with half a dozen folders in it as well as a division for the Adams Crest rental with folders in it and so on. As you pay each bill, you put the invoice in the appropriate folder noting the check number and date you paid it.

As bills come in, they can all be kept in a separate folder marked "To Be Paid." Pay them promptly and then transfer them to another folder marked "Paid Bills."

You can keep a ledger to record all monies received, from whom, the date, and the purpose. Many accountants advise that you stick all income from your rentals into a single account separate from your personal account, to avoid confusion and the chance that someone will later say you failed to properly record rental income.

Armed with your file of documented expenses, your income ledger, and your checkbook (with monthly statements and returned checks), you should be able to withstand an audit as well as be able to keep track of all your monies coming in and going out.

RENT AND EXPENSE SCHEDULES

If you have only one rental unit, this really isn't important. You can always keep track of who has paid and when in your general ledger.

However, as you add rental units, it becomes increasingly difficult to remember what the money paid was for, who paid it, and so on. Therefore, a rental income schedule with the names of tenants, their addresses, the date and amount they paid, and the purpose (laundry money income is different from rental money income) is helpful. It will let you know at a glance what money has come in, from where, and for what purpose. See the appendix for a sample rental schedule.

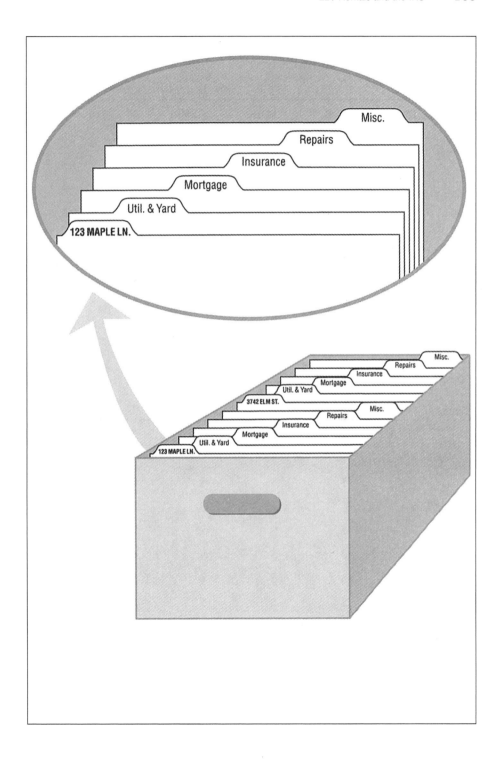

RENTAL EXPENSE SCHEDULE

Tenant	Month					
#	JAN	FEB	MAR	APRIL	MAY	JUNE
1	$	$	$	$	$	$
2	$	$	$	$	$	$
3	$	$	$	$	$	$
4	$	$	$	$	$	$
5	$	$	$	$	$	$
6	$	$	$	$	$	$
7	$	$	$	$	$	$
8	$	$	$	$	$	$
9	$	$	$	$	$	$
10	$	$	$	$	$	$
Totals						

Tenant	Month					
#	JULY	AUG	SEPT	OCT	NOV	DEC
1	$	$	$	$	$	$
2	$	$	$	$	$	$
3	$	$	$	$	$	$
4	$	$	$	$	$	$
5	$	$	$	$	$	$
6	$	$	$	$	$	$
7	$	$	$	$	$	$
8	$	$	$	$	$	$
9	$	$	$	$	$	$
10	$	$	$	$	$	$
Totals						

Similarly, a rental expense schedule showing each unit separately and the expenses paid monthly such as mortgage, utilities, maintenance, and so forth will likewise help you to keep track of where your money is going from day to day.

DEPRECIATION

One expense that no landlord/owner will want to forget is depreciation. It's the write-off your government allows on your building, but not your land. The amount you can deduct for depreciation varies depending on when you put the property into service and the type of property it is. Further, although depreciation can turn a profitable property into a losing proposition (at least on paper), it does not mean you can necessarily write off the loss in the current year.

The active/passive rules of the 1986 Tax Reform Act (under which real estate investment is defined as passive) may prevent you from writing off any loss on your real estate in the current year although you will be able to carry it forward. See later under "Tax Consequences of Using a Property Management Firm" and also check with a tax specialist to see if you qualify.

In any event, it's a good idea to keep track of your depreciation so you can see at a glance where you stand on any property. Create a separate expense folder for depreciation by property and record it annually.

COMPUTERIZING

Of course, in this day of home computers it's somewhat like being in the dark ages to not have a program that does all the above for you and much more. Even simple programs available for less than $50 will allow you to put entries in rent and expense schedules. Indeed, they will do much more, including keeping all entries on track in a general ledger, providing monthly operating statements and annual statements, even indicating which items are tax deductible and which aren't. (In a rental situation, almost everything should be tax deductible, eventually.)

Further, a good computer program can generate reports that can provide you with much useful information, such as your monthly mainte-

nance costs, your monthly mortgage expenses, your insurance costs, utility costs, and so on. It can even let you know when one of your units is
generating unusually high expenses.

Keep receipts—for every expense, every bit of income. Never trust
your memory—no one else will. Especially not the IRS!

TAX CONSEQUENCES OF USING A PROPERTY MANAGEMENT FIRM

Under the active/passive rules noted above, you may be able to write
off up to $25,000 in losses on rental real estate against your regular
income. To do this you must meet certain requirements, one of which is
that your regular income be below $100,000, to get the full write-off, and
below $150,000 to get a partial write-off. However, one of the conditions
is that you must actively participate in the management of your rental
property.

Hiring a property management firm means someone else is managing
the property, not you. However, this does not necessarily mean you are
not actively participating. You may still be able to get the write-off, provided you actively make the important decisions, such as who to rent to,
who to evict, what rental form to use, and so forth. Thus, using a property management firm does not, by itself, mean that you won't be able to
get a write-off on your rentals.

As noted above, this is a complex subject and you should check with
your tax specialist for the details.

TAX CONSEQUENCES WHEN YOU SELL

It's important to understand that the tax treatment of a rental property
is significantly different from the tax treatment of a personal residence.
Basically speaking, if you have a capital gain when you sell a rental,
you'll have to pay taxes on it. If you have a capital loss, you'll be able to
apply that loss to offset other capital gains, or to deduct it from your regular income at no more than a miniscule $3,000 a year.

Determining your actual capital gain or loss, however, can be a tough
job, particularly when you consider depreciation. In 1997 Congress passed

the Taxpayer's Relief Act, which significantly reduced the overall capital gains tax rate. However, it also added amazingly complicated rules regarding the recapture of depreciation and it created many different capital gains rates.

Therefore, unless you are very competent with tax matters, I suggest you hire a good accountant. You also may want to check into my book, *Buy or Sell Real Estate after the 1997 Tax Act* (Wiley, 1998).

CHAPTER 23

Converting Your Home into a Rental

Why would you want to convert your home into a rental? There are many reasons. You might be buying a new home and be unable to sell your old one, at least at a price you want. Yet, you must keep on making those mortgage payments on the old home. The obvious answer is to convert it into a rental. Or perhaps you bought a home with the intention of moving in, but circumstances changed and now you can't, or don't want to. Again, converting to a rental may be the answer.

However, not all properties make good rentals. Some are more suited to it than others. In this chapter we'll look at some of the factors that determine how good a rental a property will be. We'll also consider whether or not you really want to become a landlord.

IS YOUR PROPERTY SUITABLE FOR RENTING?

Can't every property be rented out, you might ask? Every property certainly can, at some price and at some risk of damage. The problem is that some properties command smaller rental rates and/or offer greater risks. Following are some of the concerns.

The House with a Pool

You may feel that a pool is a great advantage. I know that when I initially purchased properties as rentals, I used to think it was a big plus. A pool meant I could always get more rent.

However, there are a growing number of homeowners and now landlords who realize the problems that a swimming pool produces often exceeds its benefits. Thus, in many markets the pool is not a plus, but at best a "wash," and at worst a negative feature. Nevertheless, in sunbelt states it is true that you can often rent out a home with a pool quicker and for more money than a home without one.

The pool may mean higher taxes and higher insurance rates. Higher rent may well not translate into higher income.

The Very Old House

Houses, in one sense, are like cars—they deteriorate over time. When a house is new—under seven years of age, very little goes wrong with it. By the time it's a teenager, however, important areas begin causing trouble such as water heaters, roofs, and appliances. As a house gets into its twenties and thirties, there are additional problems with the heating/air conditioning system, plumbing, and especially cracking in walls and ceilings from a settling foundation. At forty, however, it may need replacement of the entire plumbing system (converting from rusting galvanized steel to copper), electrical system (converting from a two wire to a three wire grounded system), complete roof replacement, foundation repair, driveway replacement, and so on.

It's true that these expenses may occur whether you're living in the property or renting it out. However, with you living in it, you can "nurse it along," making do with old and decrepit features. When you're renting out, however, you must be sure the property is habitable and that it meets minimum public health and safety standards—unless, of course, you want your specialty to become slumlord, a heading not covered in this book.

When the air conditioning or the heating systems go out, the tenant wants them fixed immediately, and that usually means complete replacement. On the other hand, if you were living in the property you might deal with the heat or cold for a few weeks until a less expensive repair part could be found. The same holds true for leaking roofs, electrical systems that go down, plumbing that stops up, and so forth. No tenant will put up with what you might put up with. All of which says that maintenance and repair costs mean it's more expensive to rent out an older house.

Again, I recognize that many landlords disagree here and feel that a well maintained, well located older home could do very well as an investment rental. Perhaps so; however, my experience is otherwise.

The Poorly Located House

Everyone knows that location is the most important aspect of real estate. What few realize, however, is that a great location for a home to buy or sell does not necessarily make for a great home to rent out.

Properties that are close to work sites, shopping, bus lines, and so on usually make good rentals. On the other hand, being very close to these might make it more difficult to sell the house.

On the other hand, a house located far out in the woods may be an idyllic setting for someone buying a home and wanting a romantic location. But someone wanting to rent may not want the hassle of a long drive and the upkeep of a woodsy location.

In general, single-family homes, apartments, condos, duplexes, and almost all other kinds of residential rental property do best as rentals in an urban or suburban setting that is clean, relatively crime-free, and newer. Houses that are far out, that are in high crime areas, that have difficult access to freeways or bus routes, do less well.

The High-Maintenance House

As a homeowner, you may be willing to spend several hours a week watering the lawns and shrubs. I can almost guarantee your tenants won't bother. If your house has automatic sprinklers, drip or other watering systems, it's a big plus as a rental. If everything has to be done manually, it's a minus.

Big yards are great for big families, particularly when you live on the property. But if you're renting it out, big yards attract big families, which means extra wear and tear on your property. Also, there's the matter of who is going to mow the lawns, trim the shrubs, rake the leaves . . . you get the idea.

Houses with big yards tend to be a minus for landlords. Either you're going to be fighting the tenants to get the work done or you're going to have to hire a gardening service, which can cost a substantial amount of money. Hiring a gardening service, however, is a plus when finding a tenant and often allows you to charge a slightly higher rent. It rarely, however, is high enough to pay for the entire gardening service. As noted in an earlier chapter, houses with big yards also tend to be costly in terms of water.

In summary, try to avoid converting your residence to a rental if it has a pool, is old and rundown, is far off the beaten track, or has a high-maintenance yard. If you do convert with these negative features, you may end up with a substantial negative cash flow on the property.

On the other hand, if your home is newer, well located, and has no pool or big yard, it may make an ideal rental.

When You're the New Owner

Some people think that buying an existing rental filled with tenants is a plus. For example, you buy a six-unit apartment building fully leased. You don't have to worry about finding tenants; you just sit back and collect the rents, right?

Maybe! Depending on how careful you were in your purchase, the terms of your sales contract, and your own investigative efforts, you could have purchased anything from a nightmare to a gold mine. In this chapter we're going to consider some of the ramifications of buying pre-leased properties.

WHO HAS THE DEPOSITS?

This is probably the biggest area of conflict. Chances are that every tenant in the property you're buying paid a deposit(s) to the former owner. But how big was the deposit, and who now has the money?

If you're taking on a large property, say a hundred rental units and the deposits were $750 apiece, you're talking about $75,000. That's serious money; not something you leave to chance. Even if it's just a single family house that's rented out, there could be $1,000 or more in deposit money somewhere out there. If you wait until after you make the purchase to go after the money, you may never find it and may, indeed, ultimately be responsible for paying it back out of your own pocket. The time to track it down is beforehand.

WHO HAS THE LAST MONTH'S RENT?

The same holds true for the last months' rents. If the property is leased, chances are the tenants have paid their last month's rents up front. The previous landlord has the money, but unless it's placed into escrow or otherwise handled as part of your purchase transaction, you may never see it.

L A N D L O R D ' S   S T O R Y

Sally was purchasing a 14-unit apartment house that was fully rented except for one unit. She had a clause inserted in the sales agreement that the seller was to turn over to her all deposits and last months' rents. Further, she had the right to secure an inventory of the funds. However, the seller said there were no deposits and all the tenants were on a month-to-month basis, none having paid a last month's rent. Hence, there was nothing to turn over. Further, although he had signed rental agreements with all of them, he could not produce them. He said they had somehow gotten misplaced.

So, Sally went door-to-door in the building, introducing herself as the person who was buying the property and asking the tenants about rental agreements, deposits, and last months' rents. Surprisingly, nearly all of the tenants had a copy of their rental agreements. She found that five of the tenants had leases and had paid the last month's rents up front. Further, all of them claimed to have put up cleaning/security deposits of one kind or another. As the new owner, she would be responsible for one day returning these funds.

Sally inventoried the monies and then presented her inventory to the seller. It came to more than $12,000. She said that was owed to her in cash, as part of the deal. The seller said, "No way!" He at first disputed the claims of tenants about deposits and last months' rents, then said that they had indeed put up money, but it was a much lower figure. In any event, he said he had spent it all and wasn't about to sweeten the sale by $12,000. Sally pointed out that he was obligated to come up with the money, or they had no deal. After all, she wasn't going to pay $12,000 extra for the property just because he had taken the deposits and last month's rents and spent them.

Eventually they reached a compromise, part cash and part better terms on a mortgage the owner was carrying back. Sally got her building and took care of the deposits and the last months' rents.

The above story illustrates a way to handle deposits and last months' rents when buying an occupied rental property. Of course, you could always buy blind and take your chances later on. However, sometimes with very expensive properties, as noted earlier in the book, the combined deposits and other funds held for tenants can be as large or larger than the purchase down payment! It's not something you want to just let go.

GIVING NOTICE OF A CHANGE IN OWNERSHIP

After the purchase, it's important to formally let the tenants know that you're the new owner and to inform them of the way you intend doing business. The best way to accomplish this that I have found is by a formal letter. Ideally, you would have a sign-off letter from the former landlord and a sign-on letter by you, the new landlord. The idea here is to let the tenants know what's happening and to reassure them that there is a continuity of management and that their interests are protected. See the appendix for "change in ownership" sample letters.

The old landlord's letter need only be short and sweet. It lets them officially know that the building has changed hands, and that you are the new owner and will be contacting them soon. I suggest you write it yourself and have the old landlord sign it. Then you can mail it to the tenants. (If you leave it to the old landlord to do, it may never get done.)

You should include the following in the new landlord's letter:

- Introduce yourself.
- State that you have your own rental agreement that you will want the tenants to sign.
- State that you are responsible for return of deposits and last months' rents and ask the tenants to come forward with copies of their rental agreements, cancelled checks, or other evidence of having paid such deposits.
- Indicate how you intend to collect the rent in the future.
- Give tenants your correct address and phone number so they know where to send the rent and how to contact you.

CHANGING RENTAL AGREEMENTS

One thing that you will most certainly want to do is to begin using your own rental agreement with the tenants. However, you cannot simply step in and change rental agreements. You are bound by the agreement signed by the previous landlord. If it's a lease, you will have to wait until the lease term is up to change it, or offer the tenant some incentive—such as reduced rent, a few weeks' free rent, a better apartment—to change it sooner.

With a standard month-to-month agreement, you can usually change it with appropriate notice, normally 30 days. However, you will need the tenants to sign your new agreement before it becomes effective.

Sometimes a tenant will refuse to sign your new agreement and insist on staying put under the previous landlord's agreement. Perhaps there's a clause in yours that the tenant objects to. Your choices are either to change your rental agreement, which you probably won't want to do, or to ask the tenant to move. My suggestion is that if you value the tenant, you play it carefully and compromise as much as possible.

CHANGES IN RENT

When buying a rental property, the buyer often has it in mind to raise rents. After all, the value of such property is normally determined by the amount of income it produces. Raise rents and you've increased your equity, sometimes quite substantially.

If you feel that the market justifies higher rents than are currently being paid by tenants, I suggest you raise them as soon as possible, preferably within the first three months. (Of course with leases, you will have to wait until the lease term runs out to raise the rent.) The tenants will understand that the rents are being raised as part of the change in ownership and will either accept it or move. If you've checked the market carefully, they'll quickly see that the rents are only being raised to realistic levels and most will stay. Nevertheless, anytime you raise rents you always run the risk that some tenants will move rather than pay.

A HIGHER LAST MONTH'S RENT

With leases, the tenants will have probably paid the last month's rent in advance. However, you cannot raise the rent during the term of the lease, unless there is a specific clause in the lease allowing this. Further, the total amount of money to be paid over the term is usually specified. Thus, you can't increase the last month's rent for a lessee, even though other tenants may be paying more now.

Where this really becomes an issue is with a tenant who originally rented on a lease, stayed past the expiration of the lease and is now on a month-to-month basis. That tenant, through several rent increases, may now be paying $1,000 a month, although he or she originally put up only $750 for the last month's rent. Can you now insist on the extra $250 when the tenant decides to move and the last month issue comes up?

It depends on how your original lease was written. But in any event, I can guarantee you that the tenant is not going to look with pleasure upon coming up with that extra $250. In fact, most tenants will fight you tooth and nail over the money.

I suggest you calmly ask the tenant for the money and explain why it's owed to you. However, if the tenant protests strongly, I then suggest that either you compromise, accepting half, or if it's only one tenant, write it off. Sometimes the hassle just isn't worth it

GETTING COPIES OF KEYS

Ideally the previous landlord was well organized and had a separate set of duplicate keys for each rental unit. In the real world, however, the landlord may actually have been a complete dud when it came to keeping track of little things like keys. He may only have had a master. In a worst case scenario, the landlord may not have keys at all to turn over to you!

Keep in mind that you must have keys to each rental unit you manage. There could be a fire or other emergency requiring your gaining immediate access to the unit. Without a key your only recourse would be to break the door down. Thus, you will have the unpleasant job of going to each tenant and asking them for their keys so you can make a duplicate set. If they are hesitant to give them up, you can point out why you need them and what you would have to do if you didn't get them. I can't think of a single tenant I've known who would rather have his or her door knocked down rather than give up a key. Nevertheless, should a tenant still refuse, you may have to get an attorney to press this issue. You can't compromise here—you must have keys to all your rental units.

GETTING THE TENANTS TO SIGN YOUR RENTAL AGREEMENT

You may not have much information on the existing tenants. Therefore, before you have them sign a new rental agreement, you should have them fill out an information sheet. You can use the sample rental application form found in the appendix, although I wouldn't insist on all of the financial information. After all, they are already living in the property.

You need to obtain information on the following:

- What their rental term is and type of agreement.
- Number of occupants, names, ages, and pets.
- Where they work and the type of cars they have.
- Who to call in an emergency.
- Which personal property (appliances, wall coverings, and so on) belongs to them.
- How much they put up for deposits/last month's rents as evidenced by rental agreements, canceled checks, and so on.

Hint: You can get information about existing tenants' finances in part by noting the bank and account number on the check by which they pay and keeping that information for future reference. (But remember, unless they authorize it in writing, you cannot do credit checks on them.)

Early on, give a copy of your rental agreement to each tenant, along with a date by which you want it signed, keeping in mind the limitations noted above plus any other limitations imposed by local or state ordinance. Once you have the information on a tenant, you can call, perhaps a week before you want the agreement signed, and ask if the tenant has any questions or doesn't understand anything. Finally, make a date to come and have a filled out (by you) agreement signed by the tenant.

Getting a new owner may be stressful to the tenants. Your businesslike handling of the transition should make your new tenants feel secure.

The following forms are designed to give an overview of the typical forms used in property management. You should be aware that all or part of any form may not apply in your circumstances or be appropriate for your state or local area. It is suggested that before using any form, you have it checked out and customized by a competent attorney. The author and publisher assume no responsibility for the legality or appropriateness of use of these forms.

RENTAL AGREEMENT

> **CAVEAT** *Portions of the following rental agreement may not apply to your circumstances or may not be legal in your state or area. Do not use it as it is. Take it to a competent attorney in your area so that it may be customized for your state and locale and for your particular needs. The author and publisher assume no responsibility for the legality, appropriateness, or timeliness of this agreement.*

TENANCY AGREEMENT
MONTH-TO-MONTH/LEASE

THIS DOCUMENT IS INTENDED TO BE A LEGALLY BINDING AGREEMENT. READ IT CAREFULLY.

City _____

State_____

Date _____

_____ (hereinafter referred to as Landlord) agrees to rent to _____ (hereinafter referred to as tenants) _____ the property described as _____ (hereinafter referred to as the premises), together with the following personal property: carpets, window coverings, light fixtures, built-in appliances, plus the following furniture:

_____

_____

Cross out and initial one of the two following paragraphs that does not apply and fill out and initial the one that does.

☐ **LEASE** This tenancy shall commence on this ___ day of _____, ____ and terminate on (date, month, year). The total rent for this lease period is $_____. The tenants shall pay first and last month's rent in advance. Upon expiration of this agreement, the tenancy shall revert to a month-to-month tenancy at $_____ per month.

☐ **MONTH-TO-MONTH** This tenancy shall commence on (date, month, year) and may be terminated by either party by giving a 30 day WRITTEN notice of termination to the other party.

1. RENT The rent is $_____ per month payable in advance on the ____day of each calendar month. Tenants to pay rent at the office of the landlord at _____ City_____ State_____ Zip_____ or at such other place as the landlord may from time to time designate.

2. BAD CHECKS Tenants shall pay a $_____ charge for handling of each check returned by the tenants' bank for "insufficient funds" or because the account is closed. Any dishonored check shall be treated as unpaid rent. It is hereby mutually agreed that if the tenants' bank returns two checks for whatever reason, thereafter tenants shall pay all rent in the form of cash, cashier's check, or money order. Any rent not received by the fifth day after it is due shall be paid only in the form of cash, cashier's check, or money order.

3. SECURITY DEPOSIT

UNDER NO CIRCUMSTANCES SHALL THE SECURITY DEPOSIT BE USED AS THE LAST MONTH'S RENT

Tenants agree to pay a refundable security deposit of $_____ before occupying the premises. Said deposit shall be refunded within ____days along with a written accounting of disposition of said deposit after tenants completely vacate the premises provided:

A. No damage, other than normal wear and tear, has been done to the premises, the furniture, or other personal property.

B. Premises are left clean. Landlord may deduct a portion of deposit to pay for certain cleaning if premises are not left clean.

C. All utilities that are the tenants' responsibility have been paid for in full and utilities have been properly notified of the tenants' departure.

D. All keys have been returned to the landlord.

E. All other conditions and terms of this agreement have been satisfactorily fulfilled.

The landlord may use all or a portion of this security deposit as may be reasonably necessary to

A. remedy tenants' defaults in payment of rent.

B. clean premises if left uncleaned by tenants.

C. repair damages caused by tenants to premises.

If any portion of the security deposit is used during the term of the tenancy to cure a default in rent or to repair damages, tenants agree to reinstate security deposit to its full amount within _____ days of written notice delivered to tenants by landlord in person or by mail.

In addition to the above, tenants also agree to pay a refundable pet security deposit of $_____.

In addition to the above, tenants also agree to pay a refundable waterbed deposit of $_____.

In addition to the above, tenants also agree to pay a NONREFUNDABLE cleaning fee of $_____.

4. LATE FEE It is hereby agreed that if the rent is not paid by the date it is due, tenants shall pay a late fee of $_____ for each day from the rental due date until the rent is paid.

5. INSPECTION Prior to taking occupancy, tenants agree to inspect the premises and any personal property therein, and to execute an inspection sheet which shall become a part of this agreement.

6. ACCESS Tenants shall allow the landlord access to the premises at reasonable times and upon reasonable notice for the purposes of inspection, making necessary repairs, or showing the premises to prospective tenants or purchasers.

7. NOTICE If rent is not paid by the due date, landlord may serve tenants with a _____ day notice to pay rent. If landlord agrees to accept payment of rent in full and late fees after servicing notice, tenants shall in addition be subject to a $_____ fee for preparing and serving the notice.

8. OCCUPANCY The total number of adults who may occupy the premises is _____. The total number of children who may occupy the premises is _____. Their names and birthdays are:

_____

_____

_____

No pet (except an animal trained to serve the handicapped such as a seeing eye dog) shall be kept on the premises without the specific written permission of the owner. The following pet(s) may be kept. _____.

9. VEHICLES Landlord shall provide _____ covered and _____ uncovered parking areas for tenants. Tenants shall keep a maximum of _____ vehicles on the premises. All tenants' vehicles not kept in designated locations must be parked in public areas. Tenants shall park no boat, trailer, or recreational vehicle on the premises continuously for more than _____ days without prior written approval of the landlord.

10. DAMAGES AND REPAIRS Tenants agree to pay for all damages to the premises done by the tenants or their invitees. Tenants agree not to paint, paper, alter, redecorate or make repairs to the dwelling, except as provided by law, without first obtaining the landlord's specific written permission.

Landlord agrees to undertake as soon as possible any and all repairs necessary to make the premises habitable and to correct any defects which are hazardous to the health and safety of the occupants, upon notification by tenants of the problem. If the landlord cannot reasonably complete such repairs within three days, he (she) shall keep tenants informed of the work progress.

All requests by tenants for service and repairs, except in the case of an emergency, are to be in the form of writing. Tenants agree to keep the premises in good order and condition and to pay for any repairs caused by their negligence or misuse or that of their family or invitees.

It is mutually agreed that it is the tenants' responsibility to repair certain items, such as windows broken or damaged subsequent to tenants' occupancy, at tenants' expense. If tenants are unable or unwilling to repair broken or damaged windows within a reasonable period of time, landlord may make such repairs and charge tenants. The cost of the repairs must not exceed the lowest bid by a competent worker.

As of occupancy, landlord warrants that all plumbing drainage is in good working condition. Tenants thereafter agree to pay for removing all stoppages caused for any reason except for roots, defective plumbing, backup from main lines, or undefined causes as determined by the plumber who clears the line.

11. USE The premises are to be used only as a residence. No commercial use is allowed. The tenants shall have the right to quiet enjoyment of the premises. The tenants agree not to disturb, annoy, endanger, or inconvenience neighbors nor use the premises for any immoral or unlawful purpose, nor violate any law ordinance nor commit waste or nuisance upon or about the premises. No waterbed may be used on the premises without the prior written consent of the landlord.

12. UTILITIES Landlord shall pay for the following utilities _____
_____ Tenants shall be responsible for opening, closing, and paying all costs for the following utilities_____
If the tenants are responsible for trash, the tenants shall obtain and maintain trash and garbage service from the appropriate utility company.

13. YARD MAINTENANCE Landlord shall be responsible for maintaining all common areas. Tenants shall be responsible for maintaining _____.
With regard to areas tenants are to maintain, they shall be kept clear of rubbish and weeds. Lawns, shrubs, and surrounding grounds shall be kept in reasonably good condition. In the event tenants do not maintain premises in reasonably good condition, landlord at his option may provide gardening service at $_____ per month to be paid for by tenants. Landlord shall be responsible for installation, repair, and replacement of all below-ground sprinkler systems.

14. INSURANCE The landlord shall obtain fire insurance to cover the premises. Tenants are aware that landlord's insurance does not cover tenants' personal property and they are encouraged to secure a tenants' insurance policy.

In the event of a fire or casualty damage caused by tenants, they shall be responsible for payment of rent and for repairs to correct the damage. If a portion of the premises should become uninhabitable due to fire or casualty damage due to no fault of the tenants, they shall not be responsible for payment of rent for that portion. Should the entire premises be uninhabitable due to no fault of the tenants, no rent shall be due until premises shall be made habitable again. The landlord shall reserve the right to determine whether premises or a portion thereof is uninhabitable.

15. HAZARDOUS MATERIALS Tenants agree not to keep or use on the premises any materials which an insurance company may deem hazardous or to conduct any activity which increases the rate of insurance for the landlord.

16. NEGLIGENCE Tenants agree to hold the landlord harmless from claims of loss or damage to property and injury or death to persons caused by the negligence or intentional acts of the tenants or their invitees.

17. EMERGENCIES In the event of an emergency invoiving the premises, such as a plumbing stoppage, the tenants shall immediately call the landlord at _____ or other phone number as the landlord may from time to time designate, and report problem. In an emergency the landlord may enter the property without notice.

18. DELAY If the landlord shall be unable to give possession of the premises on the day of the commencement of this agreement by reason of the holding over of any prior occupant of the premises or for any other reasons beyond the control of the landlord, then tenants' obligations to pay the rent and other charges in this agreement shall not commence until possession of the premises is given or is available to tenants. Tenants agree to accept such abatement of rent as liquidated damages in full satisfaction of the failure of landlord to give possession of said premises on agreed date and further agree that landlord shall not be held liable for any damages tenants may suffer as a consequence of not receiving timely possession. If such delay exceeds _____ days from the commencement date, this agreement shall be considered void.

19. SUBLETTING Tenants shall not sublet, assign, or transfer all or part of the premises without the prior written consent of the landlord.

20. RULES Tenants shall comply with all covenants, conditions, and restrictions that apply to the premises. The tenants shall comply with all rules of a homeowner's association that apply to the premises.

21. ATTORNEY'S FEES If either party brings action to enforce any terms of this agreement or recover the possession of the premises, the prevailing party shall/shall not (cross out wording not desired and initial change) be entitled to recover from the other party his costs and attorney fees.

22. RESPONSIBILITY TO PAY RENT All undersigned tenants are jointly and severally (together and separately) liable for all rents incurred during the term of this agreement. (Every member is equally responsible for the payment of the rent.) Each tenant who signs this agreement authorizes and agrees to be the agent of all other occupants of the premises and agrees to accept, on behalf of the other occupants, service of notices and summons relating to tenancy.

23. SUBSTITUTION OF TENANTS In the event one tenant moves out and is substituted by another, the new tenant shall fill out an application and tenancy shall be subject to the approval of the landlord. No portion of the cleaning deposit will be refunded until the property is completely vacated.

24. HOLD OVER If after the date of termination of tenancy, tenants are still in possession of premises, they will be considered holding over and agree to pay rental damages at the rate of 1/30th of their then-current monthly rent per day of hold over.

25. OTHER CONDITIONS Each provision herein containing words used in the singular shall include the plural where the context requires. If any item in this agreement is found to be contrary to federal, state, or local law, it shall be considered null and void and shall not affect the validity of any other item in the agreement. The waiver of any breach of any of the terms and conditions of this lease shall not constitute a continuing waiver or a subsequent breach of any of the terms or conditions herein. The foregoing constitutes the entire agreement between the parties and may be nullified or changed only in writing and signed by both parties. Both parties have executed this lease in duplicate and hereby acknowledge receipt of a copy on the day and year first shown above. Time is of the essence in this agreement.

TENANTS ACKNOWLEDGE RECEIPT OF THE FOLLOWING:

☐ Move-in inspection sheet
☐ Homeowner's rules and regulations
☐ Entry key
☐ Community pool key
☐ Remote garage door opener
☐ Security gate card #_____
☐ Lead paint notice
☐ Smoke detector in operating condition
☐ Door lock notice
☐ Laundry room key
☐ Other _____

Tenant_____
Tenant_____
Landlord_____
Landlord_____

3-DAY NOTICE TO PAY OR QUIT

TO: _____
_____
_____
_____

You are hereby notified that the amount of $_____ is now due and payable representing rent due from ___/___/___ until ___/___/___ for the property described as _____ along with all storage and garage areas.

Demand is hereby made that you pay said rent IN FULL within three (3) days or quit the premises. You are further notified that if you fail to pay or quit, legal proceedings will be instituted against you to terminate your rental agreement or lease, to recover possession of said premises and to recover rents, court costs, attorney fees, and damages as specified in your rental agreement or lease.

NO PART PAYMENT OF RENT WILL BE ACCEPTED

Dated this _____day of_____, _____

Signed_____
Owner or owner's representative

- -

AFFIDAVIT OF SERVICE

State of _____ County of_____

I, _____, declare under penalty of perjury that I served the above notice on the tenant named above on the _____day of _____, _____ in the following manner:

☐ By handing of a copy thereof to the above named tenant.

☐ By delivering of a copy thereof to _____, a person above the age of 18 residing at the above premises.

☐ By posting a copy thereof in a conspicuous place on the above premises, no one being in actual possession thereof.

☐ By sending a copy thereof by certified mail to the tenant at his place of residence.

State of _____, County ss:

Subscribed and sworn to before me this _____ day of _____, _____
_____Notary Public

Notary Seal   Signed_____

RENTAL APPLICATION FORM

APPLICANT(S)_____

PROPERTY ADDRESS: _____

APPLICANT'S NAME: _____

SOCIAL SECURITY #: _____   DRIVERS LIC.: _____

CO-APPLICANT: _____

SOCIAL SECURITY #: _____   DRIVERS LIC.: _____

NAMES AND RELATIONSHIPS OF OTHER OCCUPANTS

_____   AGE: _____

_____   AGE: _____

PETS: _____

AUTOS: MAKE: _____   MODEL: _____   LICENSE: _____

        MAKE: _____   MODEL: _____   LICENSE: _____

HOUSING INFORMATION

CURRENT ADDRESS: _____

   YEARS: _____ MO: _____ REASON FOR LEAVING: _____

CURRENT PHONE #: _____

CURRENT LANDLORD/MANAGER: _____

   PHONE: _____

PREVIOUS ADDRESS: _____

   YEARS: _____ MO: _____ REASON FOR LEAVING: _____

FORMER LANDLORD/MANAGER: _____ PHONE: _____

EMPLOYMENT

EMPLOYER: _____ OCCUPATION: _____

YEARS: _____ SUPERVISOR: _____ PHONE: _____

PREVIOUS EMPLOYER: _____ OCCUPATION: _____

YEARS: _____ SUPERVISOR: _____ PHONE: _____

SPOUSE'S EMPLOYER: _____ OCCUPATION: _____

YEARS: _____ SUPERVISOR: _____ PHONE: _____

INCOME AND SAVINGS

MONTHLY GROSS INCOME: _____

SPOUSE'S MONTHLY GROSS: _____

OTHER INCOME: _____

CHECKING ACCNT: _____ BRANCH: _____

#: _____ LENGTH: _____

SAVINGS ACCNT: _____ BRANCH: _____

#: _____ LENGTH: _____

REFERENCES

PERSONAL REFERENCE: _____

   RELATIONSHIP: _____ PHONE #: _____

PERSONAL REFERENCE: _____

   RELATIONSHIP: _____ PHONE #: _____

IN EMERGENCY CONTACT:

   RELATIONSHIP: _____ PHONE #: _____

   RELATIONSHIP: _____ PHONE #: _____

   RELATIONSHIP: _____ PHONE #: _____

CREDIT

MAJOR CREDIT CARD: _____ #: _____ BAL: _____

MAJOR CREDIT CARD: _____ #: _____ BAL: _____

CREDIT REFERENCE: _____ PHONE #: _____

HOW MANY PEOPLE WILL OCCUPY THIS RENTAL UNIT? _____

NAMES OF OTHER OCCUPANTS: _____

HAVE YOU EVER BEEN EVICTED? _____

HAVE YOU EVER FILED BANKRUPTCY? _____

I HAVE READ THIS ENTIRE APPLICATION AND ALL OF THE INFORMATION I HAVE GIVEN IS TRUE AND CORRECT. I HEREBY GIVE PERMISSION TO LANDLORD TO VERIFY ABOVE INFORMATION, INCLUDING A CREDIT CHECK.

DATE: _____

SIGNED BY APPLICANT: _____

SIGNED BY CO-APPLICANT: _____

PROPERTY INSPECTION SHEET

Date_____

Property Address _____

Tenants' Names _____

_____

Landlord's Name _____

LIVING ROOM, DINING ROOM, FAMILY ROOM, LOFT,
BREAKFAST ROOM

(Use separate sheet for each room—circle room to which sheet applies)

Item	Condition on Arrival	Condition on Departing
		Tenants are responsible for damage beyond normal wear and tear and for areas not cleaned.
Floor Coverings		
Walls and Ceiling		
Light Fixtures		
Windows and Screens		
Window Rods and Coverings		
Doors (including hardware)		
Slider and Screen Door		
Fireplace and Equipment		
Other		

Dated_____

Signed Landlord_____

Signed Tenant_____

KITCHEN

Item	Condition on Arrival	Condition on Departing
		Tenants are responsible for damage beyond normal wear and tear and for areas not cleaned.
Floor Coverings		
Cupboards		
Walls and Ceilings		
Windows and Screens		
Window/Slider Coverings		
Doors Including Hardware		
Light Fixtures		
Counter Surfaces and Makeup		
Sink Faucets		
Garbage Disposal		
Stove Burners		
Fan		
Stove Light		
Clock		

Dated_____

Signed Landlord_____

Signed Tenant_____

Item	Condition on Arrival	Condition on Departing
Oven Heating Elements		
Broiler		
Light		
Sink Drain		
Dishwasher		
Other		

BATHROOM

Item	Condition on Arrival	Condition on Departing
		Tenants are responsible for damage beyond normal wear and tear and for areas not cleaned.
Floor Covering		
Walls & Ceiling		
Shower & Tub (Doors, tracks)		
Toilet		
Plumbing Fixtures Windows & Screens		
Doors & Hardware		

Dated_____

Signed Landlord_____

Signed Tenant_____

Item	Condition on Arrival	Condition on Departing
Light Fixtures		
Sink & Counter		
Fan		
Misc.		

BEDROOM
(Use separate sheet for each bedroom)

Item	Condition on Arrival	Condition on Departing
		Tenants are responsible for damage beyond normal wear and tear and for areas not cleaned.
Floor Covering		
Walls & Ceiling		
Closet, Doors & Track		
Windows & Screens		
Window Coverings		
Doors and Hardware		
Light Fixtures		

Dated_____

Signed Landlord_____

Signed Tenant_____

Item	Condition on Arrival	Condition on Departing
Fireplace & Equipment		
Gas Valve		
Misc.		

HALLWAY AND ENTRYWAY

Item	Condition on Arrival	Condition on Departing
		Tenants are responsible for damage beyond normal wear and tear and for areas not cleaned.
Floor Coverings		
Walls & Ceiling		
Closet Doors		
Light Fixtures		
Air Conditioning & Heating Filters		
Smoke Alarms		
Other		
Utility Room		
Floor Covering		

Dated_____

Signed Landlord_____

Signed Tenant_____

Item	Condition on Arrival	Condition on Departing
Walls & Ceiling		
Light Fixtures		
Gas or Electric Service		
Other		

GARAGE

Item	Condition on Arrival	Condition on Departing
		Tenants are responsible for damage beyond normal wear and tear and for areas not cleaned.
Washer Faucet		
Washer Drain		
Water Softener		
Furnace & Filter		
Air Conditioner		
Light Fixtures		
Floor Type and Condition		
Tools & Equipment		

Dated_____

Signed Landlord_____

Signed Tenant_____

YARD

Item	Condition on Arrival	Condition on Departing
	FRONT	*Tenants are responsible for damage beyond normal wear and tear and for areas not cleaned.*
Sprinklers		
Water Bibs		
Lawn		
Entry Light		
Walkway And Driveway		
Wall/Fence		
Garage Door		
Door Opener (Includes Remotes)		
Entry Door		
Door Bell		
Other		

Dated_____

Signed Landlord_____

Signed Tenant_____

Item	Condition on Arrival	Condition on Departing
	SIDE	*Tenants are responsible for damage beyond normal wear and tear and for areas not cleaned.*
Sprinklers		
Water Bibs		
Lawn		
Light Fixture		
Walkway		
Wall/Fence		
Door		
Other		

Item	Condition on Arrival	Condition on Departing
	REAR	*Tenants are responsible for damage beyond normal wear and tear and for areas not cleaned.*
Sprinklers		
Water Bibs		
Lawn		

Dated_____

Signed Landlord_____

Signed Tenant_____

Item	Condition on Arrival	Condition on Departing
Light Fixture		
Walkway		
Wall/Fence		
Door		
Patio		
Patio Cover		
Other		

Dated_____

Signed Landlord_____

Signed Tenant_____

MOVE-OUT INSTRUCTIONS SHEET

Dear Tenant:

At some point you will be moving from the premises you now occupy. In order to help make that move easier and to avoid confusion, I have prepared the following instructions. They will let you know what's expected of you on move-out according to the terms of your rental agreement.

WHAT IS PROPER NOTICE?

If you have a month-to-month tenancy, you are required by the terms of your rental agreement to give a minimum of ___ days notice before moving. That notice:

1. should be in writing (see the tear out at the bottom).

2. should give the exact date you intend to move.

3. should designate the move-out date; that date should be thirty days from your last rent payment. For example, if you pay on the first, you should plan to move on the first of the following month.

If your plans change and you cannot move out on the day you have designated, please let me know as soon as possible and I will try to make arrangements for you to stay longer. Be aware, however, that in many cases new tenants will waiting to move in. Also, you will be charged for any additional days you stay.

WHAT RETURNING POSSESSION MEANS

You will not be considered to have moved out and returned possession of the premises until ALL of your personal property (every bit of furniture, clothing, utensils, towels, boxes and so on) has been removed from the premises including the garage, walk-ways, utility room, and any other areas you occupy; and you have returned ALL sets of keys. Rent will not stop until all of your property has been removed (assuming also you have given proper notice).

Please call me at _____ at least three days in advance to make arrangements to return keys and to have a move-out inspection.

WHAT IS REQUIRED TO GET YOUR SECURITY DEPOSIT BACK

To get a complete refund of your security deposit you must leave the premises clean and without damage—normal wear and tear excepted, return keys and fulfill all the obligations of your rental agreement. If you have damaged the premises or left it unclean, a portion of your deposit may be used to pay for repairs, to clean areas that were left dirty (pay special attention to stoves, toilets, tubs, sinks, sills, and floors), and to pay for pet or other damage. Any unused portion of your security deposit will be returned within ___ days along with a complete written accounting of money spent.

If there are marks on walls, please call me first before attempting to clean them, else you could make them worse. Before shampooing carpets or cleaning wall coverings, please call me so that I can let you know which types of cleaning will work on the materials you have and will not cause damage.

YOUR RESPONSIBILITIES

It is your responsibility to call all utility companies to have service discontinued and to turn off phone, trash, and newspaper services. It is your responsibility to leave the premises in a clean and undamaged condition.

- -

Tear off at the dotted line and mail to landlord when you plan to move out.

Tenants' Name _____

Address_____

Day of month rent is paid _____

To:

Landlord's name_____

Landlord's address _____

You are hereby given notice that as per our rental agreement, we are giving you ___ days notice (___ days minimum notice is required) of our intention to move. We understand that we are responsible to pay rent until the end of the notice period.

Date of move-out _____

Signed Tenant_____

NEW OWNER'S/LANDLORD'S LETTER

Date_____

Tenants' name_____
Address_____

Dear Tenant:

As you may already know, I have purchased the property you are renting. I am writing to you by way of introduction so that you will know who I am (I plan to stop by within the next week or so to introduce myself personally) and you will have some idea of what to expect in the coming months.

You will need to change where you send your rent payments. Please make your next and all future rent payments to:
(Name) _____
(Address) _____
Rent can be paid in the form of a personal check, money order, or cashier's check. It is payable on the due date and is considered late thereafter. If you will have to be late for any reason, please contact me as soon as possible. Late rent can result in the institution of eviction proceedings.

I'm sure you're wondering about your security/cleaning deposit. I will be responsible for returning it to you. However, to ensure proper credit, could you please do something for me: fill out the information requested below and forward it, along with a copy of your old rental agreement, to me. (I use a different rental agreement and soon will be forwarding a copy for you.)

If you have any questions or concerns, please don't hesitate to call me. If not, I look forward to meeting with you in the very near future.

Sincerely,

(Landlord) _____

- -

TENANTS' QUESTIONNAIRE

PROPERTY ADDRESS_____

TENANT'S NAME _____

OTHER TENANT'S NAME _____

NUMBER OF ADULT OCCUPANTS _____ NAMES_____

NUMBER OF CHILDREN _____ AGES _____

NUMBER OF PETS _____ TYPE _____

NUMBER OF CARS _____ TYPE _____ LICENSE_____

TYPE _____ LICENSE_____

EMPLOYER? _____

   PHONE AT WORK _____

CURRENT RENTAL RATE $ _____

DATE RENT IS DUE _____

DATE RENT CURRENTLY PAID TO_____

DATE MOVED IN_____

DATE LEASE ENDS (UNLESS MONTH-TO-MONTH) _____

AMOUNT OF LAST MONTH'S RENT PAID $_____

REFUNDABLE SECURITY DEPOSIT PAID $ _____

OTHER DEPOSITS PAID $ _____

   PURPOSE _____

ARE ANY OF THE FOLLOWING APPLIANCES OR COVERINGS YOUR OWN
PERSONAL PROPERTY? ☐ stove ☐ washer ☐ dryer ☐ refrigerator
☐ carpeting ☐ wall coverings ☐ other_____

NOTIFY IN CASE OF EMERGENCY _____

      PHONE_____

YOUR PHONE _____

SIGNED _____

PREVIOUS OWNER'S/LANDLORD'S LETTER

Date_____
To Tenant:
Name _____
Address _____
_____

Dear Tenant:

This will serve to inform you that I have sold the property you are currently renting. The anticipated date of title transfer is _____. Please contact the new landlord/owner for needed repairs after that date. Until then, you may continue to reach me at (phone) _____.

I will be transferring your security/cleaning deposit in the amount of $_____ to the new landlord/owner who will be responsible for refunding it to you, assuming you fulfill your rental agreement obligations, upon move-out. If you have questions about this, please contact the new landlord/owner immediately.

The new landlord/owner is _____ who can be reached at _____, phone _____.

Sincerely,

(Signed previous landlord)_____

TENANTS' LETTER OF RECOMMENDATION

Date_____

To Whom It May Concern:

This will recommend (<u>insert tenants' names here</u>) to you. (Tenants' names) have been my tenants from _____ to _____. During that time the rent was always paid promptly, there was no damage done to the premises, the yard was well kept and there were no unusual problems. When they moved out, the property was left in a clean and undamaged condition.

I consider (tenants' names) to be excellent tenants.

Sincerely,

Signed (landlord) _____

LANDLORD'S RECORD OF TENANT RENTAL PAYMENTS

PAGE ONE—TENANT RECORDS

TENANT #1
TENANT NAME _____
TENANT ADDRESS _____
TENANT PHONE _____
RENTAL RATE $ _____
DEPOSITS HELD $ _____
MOVED IN _____

TENANT #2
TENANT NAME _____
TENANT ADDRESS _____
TENANT PHONE _____
RENTAL RATE $ _____
DEPOSITS HELD $ _____
MOVED IN _____

TENANT #3
TENANT NAME _____
TENANT ADDRESS _____
TENANT PHONE _____
RENTAL RATE $ _____
DEPOSITS HELD $ _____
MOVED IN _____

TENANT #4
TENANT NAME _____
TENANT ADDRESS _____
TENANT PHONE _____
RENTAL RATE $ _____
DEPOSITS HELD $ _____
MOVED IN _____

TENANT #5
TENANT NAME _____
TENANT ADDRESS _____
TENANT PHONE _____
RENTAL RATE $ _____
DEPOSITS HELD $ _____
MOVED IN _____

TENANT #6
TENANT NAME _____
TENANT ADDRESS_____
TENANT PHONE _____
RENTAL RATE $ _____
DEPOSITS HELD $ _____
MOVED IN _____

PAGE TWO—RENTAL SCHEDULE

Tenant	Month					
#	JAN	FEB	MAR	APRIL	MAY	JUNE
1	$	$	$	$	$	$
2	$	$	$	$	$	$
3	$	$	$	$	$	$
4	$	$	$	$	$	$
5	$	$	$	$	$	$
6	$	$	$	$	$	$
Totals						

Tenant	Month					
#	JULY	AUG	SEPT	OCT	NOV	DEC
1	$	$	$	$	$	$
2	$	$	$	$	$	$
3	$	$	$	$	$	$
4	$	$	$	$	$	$
5	$	$	$	$	$	$
6	$	$	$	$	$	$
Totals						

REQUEST TO VERIFY EMPLOYMENT

Name _____

Company _____

Address_____

_____

Date_____

Dear Employer:

_____ (Tenant's name) has applied to rent a house (apt./condo) from me and has given you as his/her employer. He/she says that he/she has worked for you for the past _____ years/months at a weekly salary of $_____.

I would very much appreciate it if you would verify this for me so that I can proceed with qualifying _____ (tenant's name) for the rental. Please phone me as soon as possible at _____. If you are unable to phone, please fill out the area below and return this sheet to me.

Sincerely,

Landlord

- -

☐ Verified as given   ☐ Temporary   ☐ Permanent

☐ Not verified

Comments _____

Employer _____

30-DAY NOTICE OF RENT INCREASE

Tenant: _____

Address:_____

_____

_____

Dear _____:

It has been _____ years since we last changed your rent.

As I'm sure you're aware, during that time rental rates have increased significantly in our area. And we have personally experienced increased costs for maintenance, taxes, and repairs, not to mention inflation.

Therefore, we are now forced to increase rents for the dwelling you occupy.

Effective Date Of Change:_____

New Rent:_____

We value you as tenants. If you feel you have special circumstances that you would like to discuss with us, please call our office.

Sincerely,

Landlord   Date

NOTICE TO PERFORM

Tenant: _____

Address:_____

  _____

  _____

TO: _____

_____

You are hereby notified that you are in violation of the following term(s) of your lease/rental agreement:

In violation: _____

_____

_____

You are hereby requested to correct the above violation within _____ days. If you fail to perform as directed, landlord may elect to begin legal proceedings to recover above premises and to secure damages as provided by your lease and as allowed by law.

Note: This is NOT a termination of lease notice.

Landlord   Date

NOTICE OF INTENT TO ENTER

Tenant: _____

Address:_____

_____

_____

According to your rental/lease agreement, the landlord/owner or designees may enter the property you are renting after giving a reasonable notice of at least 24 hours in advance.

You are hereby notified at least 24 hours in advance that the landlord/owner or designees intend to enter the premises you are renting at the address noted above for the purpose of:_____

Approximate time of entrance: _____

Estimated duration of stay: _____

If you will be available at the above time, please let the landlord know. However, it is not necessary that you be available on the premises at the time of entry. Landlord/owner or designees, after knocking to determine if anyone is home, will use a passkey to gain entrance.

Change of Lock Notice: If the landlord/owner or designee is unable to enter because tenant has changed or rekeyed locks, landlord will use a locksmith to open door and locks will be rekeyed. A new key will be given to tenant who will be charged for the service.

Signed: _____ Date: _____

Delivered in person by:

Signed: _____ Date: _____ Time:_____

RECEIPT FOR KEYS

Tenant: _____

Address:_____

_____

_____

Tenant acknowledges receipt of _____ keys to the above premises. Loss of any keys should be reported immediately to the landlord.

It is understood that tenant will not make any additional keys without the landlord's specific permission. It is further understood that if the tenant rekeys or adds/changes the locks, a set of new keys will immediately be given to the landlord.

Tenant acknowledges receipt of a copy of this statement.

Signed/Landlord _____ Date _____

Signed/Tenant _____ Date _____

NOTICE OF SMOKE DETECTOR

Tenant: _____

Address:_____

_____

_____

Tenant is hereby notified that the above premises has an operating smoke detector as approved by the state fire marshall and installed in accordance with regulations of the state fire marshall and local ordinances which may apply.

Tenant acknowledges that he/she has been shown location of smoke detector and has tested it to determine if it is in working condition. Tenant will immediately notify landlord if battery on smoke detector runs down (usually accompanied by a "chirping" sound).

Tenant acknowledges receipt of a copy of this statement.

Signed/Landlord _____ Date _____

Signed/Tenant _____ Date _____

NOTICE OF FIRE EXTINGUISHERS

Tenant: _____

Address:_____

_____

_____

Tenant is hereby notified that there are _____ fire extinguishers at the above premises. Fire extinguishers are located at:

_____

_____

_____

When using a fire extinguisher, stand at least six feet from fire and spray in short bursts at base of flame.

Tenant acknowledges receipt of a copy of this statement.

Signed/Landlord _____ Date _____

Signed/Tenant _____ Date _____

DISCLOSURE OF INFORMATION ON LEAD-BASED PAINT AND/OR LEAD-BASED PAINT HAZARDS

Lead Warning Statement

Housing built before 1978 may contain lead-based paint. Lead from paint, paint chips, and dust can pose health hazards if not managed properly. Lead exposure is especially harmful to young children and pregnant women. Before renting pre-1978 housing, lessors must disclose the presence of known lead-based paint and/or lead-based paint hazards in the dwelling. Lessees must also receive a federally approved pamphlet on lead poisoning prevention.

Lessor's Disclosure

(a) Presence of lead-based paint and/or lead-based paint hazards (check (i) or (ii) below):

    (i) _____ Known lead-based paint and/or lead-based paint hazards are present in the housing (explain).

    _____

    _____

    (ii) _____ Lessor has no knowledge of lead-based paint and/or lead-based paint hazards in the housing.

(b) Records and reports available to the lessor (check (i) or (ii) below):

    (i) _____ Lessor has provided the lessee with all available records and reports pertaining to lead-based paint and/or lead-based paint hazards in the housing (list documents below).

    _____

    _____

    (ii) _____ Lessor has no reports or records pertaining to lead-based paint and/or lead-based paint hazards in the housing.

Lessee's Acknowledgment (initial)

(c) _____ Lessee has received copies of all information listed above.

(d) _____ Lessee has received the pamphlet *Protect Your Family from Lead in Your Home.*

Agent's Acknowledgment (initial)

(e) _____ Agent has informed the lessor of the lessor's obligations under 42 U.S.C. 4852(d) and is aware of his/her responsibility to ensure compliance.

Certification of Accuracy

The following parties have reviewed the information herein and certify, to the best of their knowledge, that the information they have provided is true and correct.

Lessor _____ Date _____ Lessor _____ Date _____

Lessee _____ Date _____ Lessee _____ Date _____

Agent _____ Date _____ Agent _____ Date _____

RENT RECEIPT

Receipt #_____

Received from: _____

As rent payment for premises commonly known as:

_____
City   State   Zip

From:_____

To:_____.

NOTICE: There will be a $_____ service charge for all checks returned unpaid. Late rent payment charges may also be applied on returned checks.

- -

RENT RECEIPT

Receipt #_____

Received from: _____

As rent payment for premises commonly known as:

_____
City   State   Zip

From:_____

To:_____.

NOTICE: There will be a $_____ service charge for all checks returned unpaid. Late rent payment charges may also be applied on returned checks.

TENANT INSURANCE NOTICE

Tenant: _____

Address:_____

          _____

          _____

Tenant is hereby notified that while landlord carries fire and casualty insurance on the property, this covers only the premises and not the tenant's possessions. Should tenant wish to insure his/her possessions against loss from fire, water, or other source, he/she must secure his/her own tenant's policy. These are available from most insurers.

Sincerely,

_____

Landlord   Date

INDEX

A

Abandoned property, 147–51
late rental payments and,
147–48
Adults-only communities, 27
Advertising, 1–12
bulletin boards, 4
listing with agents, 5–6
move-in discounts
offered in, 12
neighborhood flier, 2–4
newspaper, 6–12
online ads, 4–5
sign, 1–2
timing of, 4
Agents, listing rentals with,
5–6
Allen wrench, 85
American Lung
Association, 63
Antidiscrimination
guidelines, 23–28
children, 26–27
federal guidelines, 23–24
gray areas, 28
income of tenants, 34
local ordinances, 25
written guidelines, 27–28
Appliances, 85
Application form, 29–37
five critical tenant tests,
30–36
sample, 219–20
verifying information
and references, 30
Arbitration clauses, 49
Asbestos, 61–63
Attorney
evictions and, 137–38
fees, 48

B

Basement, radon gas in, 64
Bathroom(s)
cleaning, 77
inspection sheet, 223–24
replacing outmoded
features in, 78
Bedroom inspection sheet,
224–25
Bounced checks, 127–28
Breakfast room inspection
sheet, 221
Breaking a lease, 44
Building codes, number of
occupants and, 26
Bulletin boards, 4
Buying an existing rental,
203–8
changing rental
agreements, 205–6
changing rents, 206
deposits, 203
giving change in
ownership notice, 205
keys and, 207
last month's rent, 204,
206–7
tenant's signatures on
new rental agreements,
208
*Buy or Sell Real Estate after
the 1997 Tax Act,* 197

C

Carbon monoxide, 64
Carpets, 76, 79, 96
Cars, per rental unit, 25
Ceilings, asbestos, 63
Change in ownership
notices, 205, 233

Children, 23, 26–27
Cleaning, in preparation for
new tenant, 75–80
carpets, 79, 96
cleaning services, 77
don't dos, 77–79
must dos, 75–77
showing property after, 80
Cleaning/security deposit,
32–33, 41
leases and, 44–46
returning, 153–60,
162–63, 171
Code upgrade insurance, 177
Collection agency, 44
eviction costs, 145
Common areas, 98
Computerized records, 195
"Consumer's Guide to
Radon Reduction," 66
Converting home to rental,
199–202
aged home, 200–1
high-maintenance house,
201–2
pools, 200
poorly located house, 201
suitability of property,
199
Credit history/report, 27,
34–36
Credit reporting agencies,
35–36

D

Death of tenant, 149–51
Demolition insurance, 177
Department of Housing and
Urban Development,
24, 65

Deposit(s)
  bank account for, 154–55
  collection of, 39–41
  interest on, 42, 155
  as last month's rent,
    158–59
  new owners and, 203
  pets and, 31–32
  receipts for, 40–41
  returning, 153–60,
    162–63, 171
  security/cleaning, 32–33,
    41, 44–46
  size of, determining,
    41–42
  walk-through inspection
    and, 89–96
Depreciation, 195
Destructive tenants, 105–9
  damage, 107–9
  messes, 106–7
Dining room inspection
  sheet, 221
Direct deposit, of rent, 126
Disabled tenants, property
  modifications and, 24
Disclosures, 57–63
  See also Health/safety
    concerns
  asbestos, 61–63
  lead, 57–61
Discrimination, avoiding
  See Antidiscrimination
  guidelines
Documentation of property
  condition, 92–96
  film and video
    documentation, 92–94
  walk-through inspection
    sheets, 94–96
Documentation of rent and
  expenses, 191

E

Earthquake insurance, 176
Employees
  safety issues involving,
    72–73
  worker's compensation,
    178–79
Employment, request to
  verify, 241

Endorsements, 177
Enter(ing) tenant's
  residence, notice of
  intent to, 247
Entryway
  cleaning/painting, 75–76
  inspection sheet, 225
EPA, 61
Equifax, 35
Eviction, 131, 137–46
  contested, 143–44
  goal, 142–43
  legal assistance, 137–38
  partial payment caution,
    144–45
  process, 138–39
  securing the premises,
    145–46
  self-help, 139–40
  serving notices, 140–42
Expenses, documentation
  of, 191–92
Experion, 35
Extended or homeowner's
  insurance, 175–76
EZ-Units, 189

F

Fair Housing Act, 23. *See
  also* Antidiscrimination
  guidelines
Fair Housing Information
  Clearinghouse, 24
Family room inspection
  sheet, 221
Fee lists, 6
Fencing, pool safety and,
  69–70
Fire extinguishers, 67–69,
  96
  notice of, 253
Fire insurance, 174–75
Fliers, advertising, 2–4
Flood insurance, 176
Floors, 76
Formaldehyde, 64–65
Forms, 209–59
  disclaimer, 209
  lead-based paint
    disclosure, 255
  move-out instructions
    sheet, 231–32

new owner's/landlord's
  letter, 233
notice of fire
  extinguishers, 253
notice of intent to enter,
  247
notice to perform, 245
notice of smoke detector,
  251
property inspection
  sheet, 221–29
receipt for keys, 249
rental agreement, 211–16
rental application form,
  219–20
rental payments,
  landlord's record of,
  238–39
rent receipt, 257
request to verify
  employment, 241
tenant insurance notice,
  259
tenants' letter of
  recommendation, 164,
  236
tenants' questionnaire,
  234
30-day notice of rent
  increase, 243
3-day notice to pay or
  quit, 217
For rent sign, 1–2

G

Garage
  gas appliances in, 71
  inspection sheet, 226
Garbage collection, 87
Garbage disposal, 85
Gas
  appliances, in garage, 71
  turn-off, 86

H

Hallway inspection sheet,
  225–26
Handicapped access, 24
Health/safety concerns,
  57–73
  asbestos, 61–63
  carbon monoxide, 64

employees, 72–73
fire extinguishers, 67–69
formaldehyde, 64–65
gas appliances in the
    garage, 71
lead, 57–61
lighting, 72
pool/spa safety, 69–70
radon gas, 65–66
security locks, 72
security peepholes, 71–72
smoke alarm, 66–67
water heater safety,
    70–71
Heaters, 64, 65
Homeowner's insurance,
    175–76
Housing and Urban
    Development,
    Department of, 24, 65
HUD, 24, 65

I

Income, of tenants, 33–34
Inflation guard, 177
Insulation, 64
Insurance, 173–80
    claims, care with, 180
    company, finding,
        179–80
    damage, special
        endorsements or
        policies for, 177
    deductibles, 179–80
    demolition/code upgrade,
        177
    earthquake/flood/storm
        endorsements or
        policies, 176
    extended or
        homeowner's, 175–76
    fire, 174–75
    inflation guard, 177
    liability, 70, 173–74
    loss of rents, 177
    notice, 259
    pool/spa and, 70
    premium savers, 180
    tenant's, 178
    vandalism, 176
    worker's compensation,
        178–79

Inspection sheet, 221–29
Interest, on deposits, 42
Internal Revenue Service,
    rental income and,
    191–97
Internet advertising, 4–5

K

Keys, 82–84
    obtaining, by new
        owners, 207
    receipt for, 82, 249
    return of, on move-out,
        163
Kitchen
    cleaning, 76
    inspection sheet, 222–23

L

Landlord associations, 36
Last month's rent, 45,
    47–48, 206–7
Late rental payments,
    121–28
Lawn sprinklers, 85–86
Lead
    in paint, 58, 59–60, 255
    in water, 58–59
Lease, 42–46, 47–48
    See also Rental
        agreement
    cleaning/security deposit
        and, 44–45
    expiration of, 45
    selling a property with a,
        44–45
Legal
    assistance, evictions and,
        137–38, 142
    fees, 48
Letter of recommendation,
    164, 236
Liability insurance, 173–74
Lighting, in common areas,
    72
Living room inspection
    sheet, 221
Location, 201
Locks
    deadbolt, 83
    giving tenants keys to,
        82–83

rekeying, 83–84
security, 72
Loft inspection sheet, 221

M

Maintenance, 97–99
    high-maintenance
        houses, 201–2
    pool/spa, 70, 200
    prompt attention to
        problems, 99
    schedule, 97–98
Month-to-month lease, 42,
    46–47, 206. *See also*
    Rental agreement
Move-in considerations
    date, 37
    discounts, 12
    getting money prior to,
        81–82
    locks and keys, 82–84
    meeting new tenants at
        the property, 82
    "presents," 84–86
    smoke alarms, 87
    turn-offs for water, gas,
        etc., 86
    utilities, 87
Move-out, 161–71
    confirmation of date of,
        164
    instructions sheet,
        231–32
    letter of
        recommendation, 164
    meeting with tenants at
        move-out time,
        164–66
    proper notice of, 161–62,
        163
    repair disputes, 169–71
    return of deposits,
        162–63, 171
    return of keys, 163
    utilities, disconnection
        of, 163
    walk-through inspection,
        166–69, 171

N

New owner's/landlord's
    letter, 233

Newspaper ads, 6–12
  abbreviations, 9–10
  discounted, 11–12
Noisy tenants, 98–99
Notice to perform, 245
Notice to quit, 141–42

O

Occupancy, number of
  occupants per house,
  25, 26
Odors, 77
Online advertising, 4–5
Ovens, 76

P–Q

Paint
  lead-based, 58, 59–60,
  255
  washable, 77–78, 111
Painting, 110–11
Paneling, 64
Parking, handicapped, 24
Partial rent payments,
  126–27
Particleboard, 65
Pay-or-quit notice, 138,
  141. *See also* Eviction
Peepholes, security, 71–72
Pets, 16, 24, 31–32
  cleaning deposits and,
  159–60
Plumber's helper, 84–85
Plumbing, 109–10
Plywood, 65
Police checks, on
  employees, 73
Pool, 200
  cleaning of, 111
  safety, 69–70
Previous owner's/landlord's
  letter, 235
"Professional tenant," 15
Property
  condition, documenting,
  92–96
  promoting, 14–15
  showing, 20–21
  uninhabitable, 119
Property inspection form,
  94–95
  sample, 221–29

Property management firm,
  183, 187–89
  tax consequences of
  using, 196
Qualifying the tenant,
  15–16

R

Radon gas, 65–66
Raising rent, 181–85
  cost-of-moving factor,
  185
  determining market rate,
  181–83
  timing of, 184
Real estate agents, rentals
  and, 5–6
Receipts, 40, 134, 257
Recommendations, 30–31
References, 29
Rent
  collection guidelines,
  134
  deductions, for work,
  113, 116–17
  direct deposit of, 126
  income, and tax
  considerations, 191–97
  insurance for loss of, 177
  landlord's record of
  tenant payments,
  238–39
  last month's, 45, 47–48,
  206–7
  late payment of, 121–28,
  147–48
  nonpaying, nonmoving,
  129–35
  partial payment of,
  126–27
  raising of, 181–85. *See
  also* Raising rent
  receipt, 134, 257
  rent and expense
  schedules, 192–94
  30-day notice of increase
  of, 243
Rental agreement, 39–55
  arbitration clauses, 49
  attorney's fees, 48
  deposit, 39–41
  lease, 42–46, 47–48

  month-to-month, 42,
  46–47
  sample, 50–55, 211–16
  unenforceable clauses,
  49
Rental history check, 36
Repair jobs, 111, 115–19
  tenants' performance of,
  and rent deductions,
  116–17
  tenants' repair rights,
  115–16
Replacement cost
  insurance, 174–75

S

Safety codes, number of
  occupants and, 26
Safety concerns. *See*
  Health/safety concerns
Security
  See also Health/safety
  concerns
  employees, 72–73
  lighting, 72
  locks, 72
  peepholes, 71–72
Security deposit, 32–33, 41
  bank account for, 154–55
  leases and, 44–46
  pets and, 159–60
  returning, 153–60,
  162–63, 171
  used as last month's rent,
  158–59
Seeing-eye dogs, 16, 24
Selling your property, tax
  consequences of,
  196–97
Showing the property,
  20–21, 80
Sign, for rent, 1–2
Smells, 77
Smoke detector, 66–67, 87,
  96
  notice of, 251
Space heaters, 64
Spa
  cleaning, 111
  safety, 69–70
Sprinklers, 85–86,
  111–12

Storm endorsements or policies, 176
Stoves, 76

T

Taxes, on rental income, 191–97
  property management firms and, 196
  selling your property and, 196–97
Tenancy agreement, 211–16
Tenant(s), 13–21, 81–88
  death of, on property, 149–51
  destructive, 105–14
  eviction of. *See* Eviction
  improvement to property by, 111–13
  insurance, 178
  late rental payments by, 121–28
  locating, 124–25
  maintenance jobs, 109–11
  making appointment to show property, 17–18
  meeting the prospective, 18–20
  minimum tenant qualifications, 16
  moving in, 81–88
  noisy, 98–99
  nonpaying, nonmoving, 129–35
  relationship with, 100–103
  responding to phone queries, 13–16
  showing the property, 20–21
Tenant guidelines, 27–28
Tenant insurance notice, 259
Tenants' questionnaire, 234
3-day notice to pay or quit, 217
Timing, advertising and, 4
Toxic materials. *See* Health/safety concerns
Toxic Substance Control Act, 65
Trans Union, 35
Trust accounts, 155

U–V

Uninhabitable property, 119
Unlawful detainer action, 141
Utilities, 87

disconnection of, 163
Vandalism insurance, 176
Verification of deposit request, 34

W–Y

Walk-through inspection, 89–96, 166–71
  cleaning deposits and, 90–91
  conducting, 95–96
  disputes over price of repairs, 169–71
  documenting property condition, 92–94
  inspection sheets, 94
Wall paneling/insulation, 64
Walls, cleaning, 76, 77–78, 111
Water
  lead contained in, 58–59
  turn-off, 86
Water heater safety, 70–71
Wood burning stoves, 64
Worker's compensation, 178–79
Yard
  inspection sheet, 227–29
  maintenance, 109, 202